JAZZ COMPOSITION
THEORY AND PRACTICE

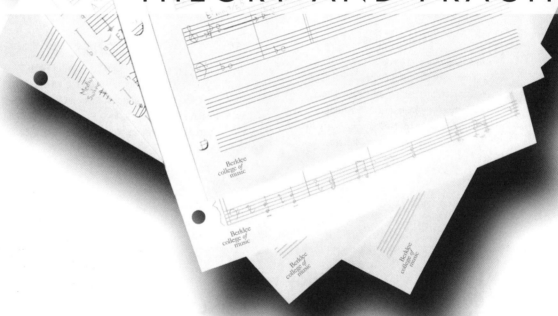

To access audio visit:
www.halleonard.com/mylibrary

Enter Code
3027-3362-0504-3018

TED PEASE

Edited by Rick Mattingly

Berklee Media

Associate Vice President: Dave Kusek
Director of Content: Debbie Cavalier
Business Manager: Linda Chady Chase
Technology Manager: Mike Serio
Marketing Manager, Berkleemusic: Barry Kelly
Senior Designer: David Ehlers

Berklee Press

Senior Writer/Editor: Jonathan Feist
Writer/Editor: Susan Gedutis
Production Manager: Shawn Girsberger
Marketing Manager, Berklee Press: Jennifer Rassler
Product Marketing Manager: David Goldberg

Cover Design: David Ehlers

ISBN 978-0-87639-001-6

1140 Boylston Street
Boston, MA 02215-3693 USA
(617) 747-2146

Visit Berklee Press Online at
www.berkleepress.com

Study with
■ **BERKLEE ONLINE**

online.berklee.edu

DISTRIBUTED BY

HAL•LEONARD®
CORPORATION
7777 W. BLUEMOUND RD. P.O. BOX 13819
MILWAUKEE, WISCONSIN 53213

Visit Hal Leonard Online at
www.halleonard.com

Berklee Press, a publishing activity of Berklee College of Music, is a not-for-profit educational publisher.
Available proceeds from the sales of our products are contributed to the scholarship funds of the college.

Printed in the United States of America

Table of Contents

Recorded Examples

Preface

My purpose in writing *Jazz Composition: Theory and Practice* is to demystify the processes involved in writing jazz tunes and in composing episodic and extended jazz works. This book is a by-product of my twenty-five years of teaching jazz composition at Berklee College of Music. Its content has been shaped by the input of my many students, by countless discussions with learned colleagues and other professionals, and by my own composing.

As a theory text, the book provides information regarding the melodic, harmonic, and rhythmic elements of jazz, along with numerous recorded music examples that demonstrate those elements. As a practice manual, the book contains a variety of music-writing exercises designed to focus on these same elements one at a time and thereby help aspirants begin producing their own effective jazz compositions.

Becoming a successful composer of jazz music will depend upon many things: the extent of your listening and playing experience, your receptivity, your time and talent, your ears, your persistence, the potential writing outlets you have, and, ideally, the guidance of a knowledgeable teacher. I hope this book will provide you with some strategies and help point the way.

Good luck!

Ted Pease
Boston, Massachusetts
January, 2003

Introduction

What is Jazz?

Trying to define jazz is like trying to describe the color green to someone who is color blind. A lot of ink has been spilled and arguments raised on this subject. My personal definitions of jazz and jazz composition are presented here not as dogma, but rather to give you some sense of where I am coming from in this book.

In my view, jazz is a unique and important American musical art form with nineteenth- and early twentieth-century African-American origins that, over the past one hundred years or so, has developed into a highly sophisticated musical idiom with improvisation, rhythmic swing, and individual expression at its core. Jazz is characterized by instrumental solos, syncopated melody and rhythm, idiomatic voicings and chord progressions, characteristic instrumentation, and a highly personalized approach to vocal and instrumental performance.

What is Jazz Composition?

Jazz composition involves writing down specific combinations of melodic, harmonic, and rhythmic elements that, in turn, produce idiomatically recognizable jazz forms (such as the blues and other song forms) or longer works in which motivic development may play an important role. Jazz composition has evolved, along with jazz performance, into a disciplined art that often evidences great emotional depth and breadth of sophistication.

When I think of jazz composers and jazz composition, I immediately think of Duke Ellington. Then other names come to mind: Billy Strayhorn, Don Redman, Jimmy Mundy, Jelly Roll Morton, Charlie Parker, Dizzy Gillespie, Tadd Dameron, Thelonious Monk, Charles Mingus, Horace Silver, George Russell, Gil Evans, Dave Brubeck, Chick Corea, Thad Jones, Herbie Hancock, Wayne Shorter, Bill Holman, Bob Brookmeyer, Jim McNeely, and Maria Schneider. These composers (and so many others) have made significant contributions to the jazz legacy, whether with memorable tunes or with elaborate extended works. This book is about what they do.

Prerequisites: What Do I Need to Know?

In order to take full advantage of this text, you need to have a working knowledge of basic music theory. You should be familiar with pitch notation in treble and bass clef, major and minor scales, modes, intervals, and chord spelling of triads and seventh chords. It will also help if you have had experience with lead sheets and/or piano sheet music, and that you have access to some "legal" fake books.

The author assumes that you have at least a modest jazz record or CD collection, and that you have been listening to major jazz practitioners, both past and present, for some time. Most important to your gaining the maximum benefit from the text is that you have had some experience *playing* jazz—or at least some experience improvising on the blues and other simple jazz forms.

Acknowledgments and Thanks

For logistical and editorial support:
Dave Kusek, Associate Vice President, Berklee Media
Debbie Cavalier, Director of Content, Berklee Media
Rick Mattingly, Editor
Susan Gedutis, Writer/Editor, Berklee Press
Shawn Girsberger, Production Manager
MusiComp, Inc., Music Engraving

My colleagues in the Jazz Composition department at Berklee College of Music:
Ken Pullig, Chair
Scott Free, Professor
Jeff Friedman, Professor
Greg Hopkins, Professor
Dick Lowell, Associate Professor
Bob Pilkington, Associate Professor
Jackson Schultz, Associate Professor
Bill Scism, Associate Professor
Phil Wilson, Professor

The quintet:
Greg Hopkins, trumpet, flugelhorn
Daryl Lowery, tenor and soprano saxophones
Tony Germain, piano
John Repucci, bass
Dave Weigert, drums

The saxophone quintet:
Larry Monroe, alto
Bruce Nifong, alto
Bill Pierce, tenor
Greg Badolato, tenor
Joe Calo, baritone

The big band:
trumpets: Jay Daly, Jeff Stout, Greg Hopkins, Ken Cervenka
trombones: Tony Lada, Phil Wilson, Rick Stepton, Pete Cirelli
woodwinds: Mark Pinto, Bruce Nifong, Greg Badolato, Bill Pierce, Joe Calo
piano: Brad Hatfield
bass: Dave Clark
drums: Joe Hunt

MIDI arranging, production, and performance of the fusion pieces (Special thanks, Emir!):
Emir Isilay

Engineers:
Big band: Don Puluse, Berklee College of Music Studios
Quintet: Bob Patton, Thin Ice Productions, North Andover, MA

Facilitators:
Ken Dorn and David Gibson of *Jazz Player* magazine
Ron Keezer of <ReallyGoodMusic.com>
The National Endowment for the Arts for funding "Suite for Jazz Band"

Mentors (special thanks for your presence and musical guidance over many years):

Herb Pomeroy
Ray Santisi
John LaPorta
Joe Viola
Robert Share

Bob Freedman
William Maloof
John Bavicchi
Richard Bobbitt
Alan Dawson

Special thanks to these musicians/jazz educators whose words and music have provided me with enlightenment and enjoyment during my career:

George Brambilla
Bob Brookmeyer
Steve Brown
Jerry Cecco
Bob Curnow
Bill Dobbins
Michael Gibbs
Bill Holman
Greg Hopkins
John LaBarbera
Alfred Lee
Everett Longstreth

Andy McGhee
Larry Monroe
Chuck Owen
Jim Progris
Michael Rendish
George Russell
Daniel Ian Smith
Al Steger
Alex Ulanowsky
James Williams
Dick Wright
Ed Xiques

Special thanks for performing my music over the years:

Daniel Ian Smith and the Big and Phat Jazz Orchestra
Larry Monroe and the Berklee Faculty Concert Jazz Orchestra
Annual Jazz Composition Department Faculty Concert: "Fall Together"
      (special thanks to Bob Pilkington and Ken Pullig)

Berklee College of Music administration:

Lee Eliot Berk, President
Gary Burton, Executive Vice President
Harry Chalmiers, Vice President Academic Affairs/Provost
Bob Myers, Associate Vice President for Institutional Research

Special thanks for my family:

My wife Lucy; my daughter Melissa; my son Gary and his family; and my daughter Allison and her family.

About the Author

Ted Pease has been a faculty member at Berklee College of Music since 1964. He is currently Distinguished Professor of Jazz Composition. Professor Pease is past chairperson of the Professional Writing Division at Berklee and past chairperson of the Jazz Composition and Arranging departments. He has authored several jazz arranging texts that have been used at Berklee for more than twenty-five years. He has received two grants in jazz composition from the National Endowment for the Arts. Eight of his compositions are featured on his CD, *Big Band Blues Celebration*. He has been recognized as an Exceptional Artist by the Massachusetts Cultural Council's Artist Grants Program. He has been a contributing writer for *Jazz Player* magazine. As a drummer with forty years of professional experience, he has performed with Herb Pomeroy, Ray Santisi, George Mraz, John LaPorta, Charlie Mariano, Toshiko Akioshi, Red Norvo, Lee Konitz, Greg Hopkins, Tony Lada, and Dick Johnson. Professor Pease is also an experienced clinician and adjudicator with more than thirty-five years' experience in jazz education.

How to Use this Book and Audio

As you study the text, listen to the related audio music examples. Listen to each example several times to get the sounds in your ear. Complete the suggested exercises and apply the various techniques. Write out these exercises carefully and check the sounds at the piano. If necessary, get a piano player to help you do this. If possible, record your examples. If you are using a computer program, you can play back your examples to see how they sound. Needless to say, an experienced teacher will be invaluable in guiding you through the text and checking your work. If possible, you should also write out individual parts and have your examples played in real time.

Analyze the tonality/modality and form of the tunes in the book. Ask yourself: Is there motivic content in the melody? Do parts of the tune repeat? Are there any distinguishing rhythm patterns in the melody? What other features of the tune are interesting? Play or sing along with the recording. What is the shape of the melody? Does the range exceed that of your voice or your instrument? Does the melody develop smoothly, or are there "hills and valleys"? Can you remember the melody later in the day? Do you find yourself singing or whistling it? If so, what is it about the melody that sticks in your mind?

Valuable supplemental resources are available to the aspiring jazz composer. If you need help regarding arranging techniques (voicings, approach techniques, instrumentation, chord-scale theory, etc.) I suggest, as a companion text to this one, *Modern Jazz Voicings* by Ted Pease and Ken Pullig, which is also published by Berklee Press. Also, check out some of the new "legal" fake books for ideas on notation and format. Sher Music Company has published several, and Hal Leonard Corporation distributes a good one.

At the end of most chapters you will find a list of source materials—tunes and compositions that deal with the subject matter at hand. Most of the tunes and compositions I have referenced were written by jazz musicians for the purpose of jazz performance. There are a few references to standards by Duke Ellington, Jerome Kern, Cole Porter, George Gershwin, and others, which have long been associated with jazz performance and which may be helpful in shedding additional light on the current topic.

If you are interested enough in jazz to have purchased this book, chances are you have been playing jazz for some time. You may even have professional playing experience. Obviously, you have been *listening* to jazz recordings and have been enthralled to one degree or another by what you have heard. You are most likely trying to replicate sounds from these recordings on your instrument. Now it's time to replicate these sounds in writing!

Review

Scales

Major

Natural Minor

Harmonic Minor
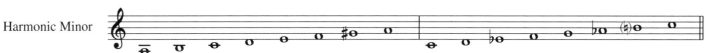

Melodic Minor

Modes

Dorian

Phrygian

Lydian

Mixolydian

Aeolian

Locrian

Tensions

Tensions are the higher functions of seventh chords. They are realized by extending chords upward past the 7th in successive intervals of a third. Thus, tensions include such functions as 9, 11, and 13 and their respective chromatic alterations (♭9, ♯9, ♯11, ♭13).

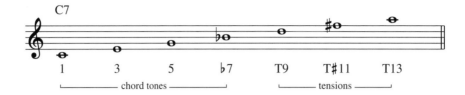

Tensions are so named because they create more dissonant intervals in the chord structure than do the chord tones alone. When tensions are used, intervals of the major and minor seventh and ninth occur.

Melodic tensions are vertically significant non-chord tones that are:

1. longer than a quarter note in duration, and/or

2. followed by a leap, and/or

3. on a strong beat preceded by a leap from below and followed by a related chord tone on a weak beat, as in 9 to 1, 11 to 3, or 13 to 5. (In classical music, this is known as an appoggiatura, or, if tied over from a note in the previous measure, a suspension.)

Medium swing

Available Tensions by Chord Type

Chord Type	Tensions							Special Situations			
	♭9	9	♯9	11	♯11	♭13	13	sus4	Maj7	#5	♭5
Major 6		√			√		(6)		√		√
Minor 6		√		√			(6)		√		
Major 7		√	rare		√		√		chord tone	rare	√
Minor(Maj7)		√		√			√		chord tone		
Minor 7	Phrygian	√		√		Aeolian	Dorian	(11)			
Minor 7(♭5)		Ionian		√		√				(♭13)	chord tone
Dominant 7	√	√	√	(sus4)	√	√	√	√		(♭13)	√
Augmented 7		√			√	(♯5)				chord tone	
Diminished 7*		√		√		√			√	(♭13)	chord tone

*Note: Tensions on diminished chords are not usually labeled by interval on lead sheets. The general consensus is that available tensions on diminished chords are those notes a whole step above a chord tone that are diatonic to the prevailing key.

Approach Notes and Other Embellishments

Approach notes have a linear melodic purpose. They are short-duration notes that move by step to chord tones or tensions. (Chord tones and tensions have a vertical melodic purpose, helping to provide focal points that are in agreement with the underlying harmony.)

Approach notes occur in melodic patterns as:
1. **passing tones (PT)**, which move stepwise between two notes of different pitch

2. **neighbor tones (NT)**, which leave and return to the same note in stepwise motion or proceed directly to a target note without preparation

3. **indirect resolution (IR)**, which consists of two notes of short and equal duration that approach the target note by step from above and below

4. **double chromatic approach (DCHR)**, which consists of two notes of short and equal duration that move by consecutive half steps to a target note

Other embellishments include **escape tones (ET)**, which interrupt the upward or downward flow of a melody by moving in the opposite direction by step and then leaping to "catch up."

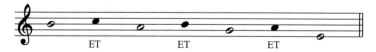

Anticipation and Delayed Attack

Rhythmic **anticipation (A)** occurs when an on-the-beat note is attacked a half beat or a whole beat early. If a chord change is involved, the chord is also anticipated.

A **delayed attack (DA)** occurs when an on-the-beat note is attacked a half beat or a whole beat late. If a chord change is involved, the chord is also delayed.

Guide Tones

Guide tones are chord tones or tensions that are voice led from one chord to a new chord tone or tension on a subsequent chord by common tone or stepwise motion. The 1 and 5 of a chord are weak guide tones because they duplicate the bass line. The 3 and 7 of a chord are the most harmonically definitive guide tones. Tensions, especially chromatically altered tensions, are the most dissonant guide tones and therefore the most unstable and dramatic.

The following example shows all of the voice-leading choices when moving from a given note in a D–7 chord to G7. (o = usual voice leading; $\bullet$ = less common)

The choice of available tensions is often aided by designated tensions in the chord symbol. In any case, you must use your ears!

FURTHER REFINEMENTS

1. Within the duration of a chord, a leap to another guide tone may occur before moving on.

2. If adjacent chords share a guide tone, you can leap between chords.

3. Compound lines are possible when two sets of guide tones "play tag" through a progression.

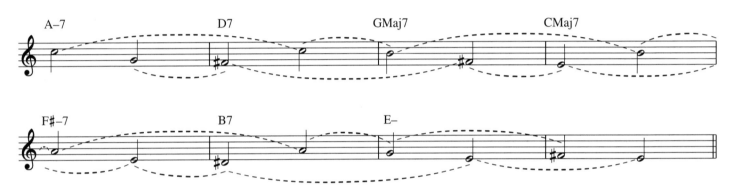

A thorough discussion of guide tone usage appears later in the book.

CHAPTER 1
Melodic Considerations

Definitions

Melody: A broad general term used in defining a succession of pitches having an established rhythm. A melody may encompass a theme that, in turn, may encompass a motif or motifs. The term "melody" is used in a variety of ways:
"This piece has a nice melody."
"The melody is played by the flute."
"This melody is angular and fragmented."
"The melody begins at letter A after the introduction."
"The melody and the harmony should agree."

Theme: A melody, or a portion of a melody, that recurs often enough in a composition that it comes to be identified with that composition.

Song: A short composition consisting of a melody, usually set to harmony, that has a beginning, middle, and end and contains lyrics (words).

Tune: In jazz parlance, the common term for a song without words. A jazz tune can usually be represented on a lead sheet.

Lead Sheet: A lead sheet depicts the melody and chord symbols of a tune. Other important features on a lead sheet may include a bass line and/or specific chord voicings for the piano.

Head: In jazz parlance, "head" is synonymous with "tune."

Harmony: A broad, general term used in defining a succession of chords in a composition. The term "harmony" is also used when describing a harmonic *system*, as in "tertian" harmony (harmony in thirds), or "quartal" harmony (harmony in fourths).

Chord: A vertical musical structure consisting of three or more pitches.

Changes: In jazz parlance, "changes" refers to the specific chord progression of a tune.

Chord Symbol: Shorthand designation of a chord, e.g., B♭7, CMaj7, etc.

Voicing: The specific positioning of pitches in a chord.

Motif: A short melodic fragment (2–5 notes), consisting of a specific pattern of pitches and rhythm. Motifs are manipulated in a composition in order to facilitate melodic development and contribute to the unity and coherence of a piece. (See example below.)

Phrase: A segment of melody that is heard as a unit but which needs other phrases in combination with it in order to present a complete musical statement. A phrase will often include an identifying motif.

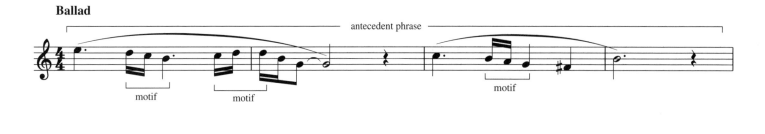

(See "Your Smile," page 135.)

Motif =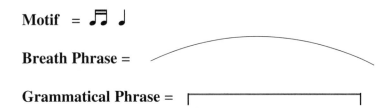

Breath Phrase =

Grammatical Phrase =

Antecedent: A musical "proposal" (open ended, as if with a comma)

Consequent: A musical "response" (closed, as if with a period)

Form Phrase: A complete musical "sentence" that represents a major subdivision of the tune. For example, if the above 8-measure melody constitutes the "a" section of a standard 32-measure tune in aaba form, we would describe the tune in general terms as "aaba form with 8-measure phrases."

EXERCISE

On the lead sheet of "Strays," identify and label:

1. the main motif (circle it each time it occurs)

2. breath phrases (with curved lines)

3. the antecedent and consequent phrases (with brackets)

Strays (for Billy Strayhorn)

Ted Pease

Melodic Rhythm

The most distinguishing characteristic of jazz melody is its rhythm. Jazz music has been associated with dancing and other body movements from the very beginning. In fact the word jazz was often used as a verb, as in "Let's jazz up that song." "Jazzing up" a song involves creating syncopations. This is accomplished by anticipating or delaying the attack of notes that would otherwise be found on the beat. The ultimate aim in "jazzing up" a melody is to make it "swing." In recorded example 2 a familiar melody by Beethoven has been "jazzed up."

Ode No. 1

Beethoven/arr. Pease

Melodic Rhythm Density as a Function of Style

The rhythmic density of a jazz melody refers to the relative number of rhythmic attacks per measure in the melody and in the piece as a whole. Rhythmic density is largely a function of style and may reflect the era in which the tune was written.

Early jazz and swing era tunes have a low to medium rhythmic density. (See "Any Friday," page 120.)

Medium Swing

Bebop tunes contain a high degree of rhythmic density. (See "Thad's Pad," page 129.)

Fast

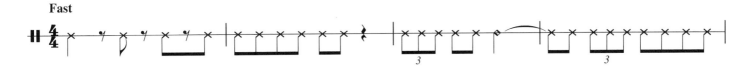

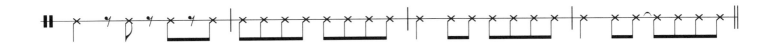

Modal tunes alternate back and forth from low to medium rhythmic density. There are liable to be numerous notes of long duration, which are used for modal emphasis. (See "Uno, Dos, Tres…," page 181.)

Medium

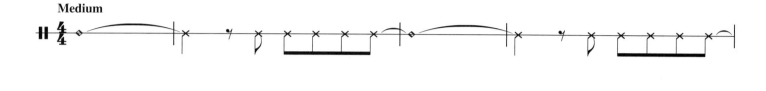

Fusion tunes use various combinations of rhythms, including rhythms with a double-time feel. Some melodies employ fragmentation while the rhythm section keeps a steady beat. (See "With All Due Respect," page 193.)

Fusion

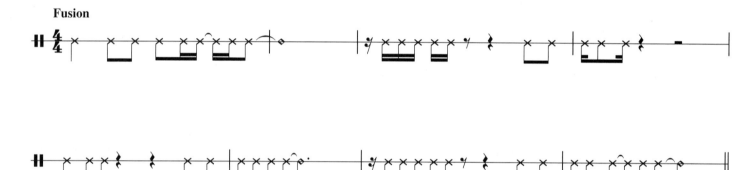

EXERCISE

1. Can you identify the well-known jazz tunes represented by the following melodic rhythms? (Answers on page 9.)

2. Circle the most prominent rhythmic motif in each.

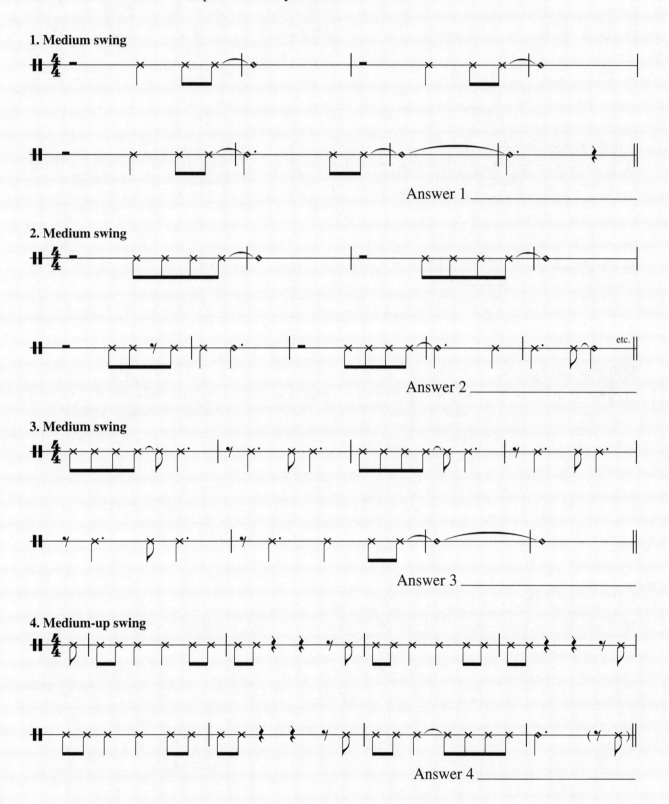

1. Medium swing

Answer 1 _____

2. Medium swing

Answer 2 _____

3. Medium swing

Answer 3 _____

4. Medium-up swing

Answer 4 _____

5. Fast swing

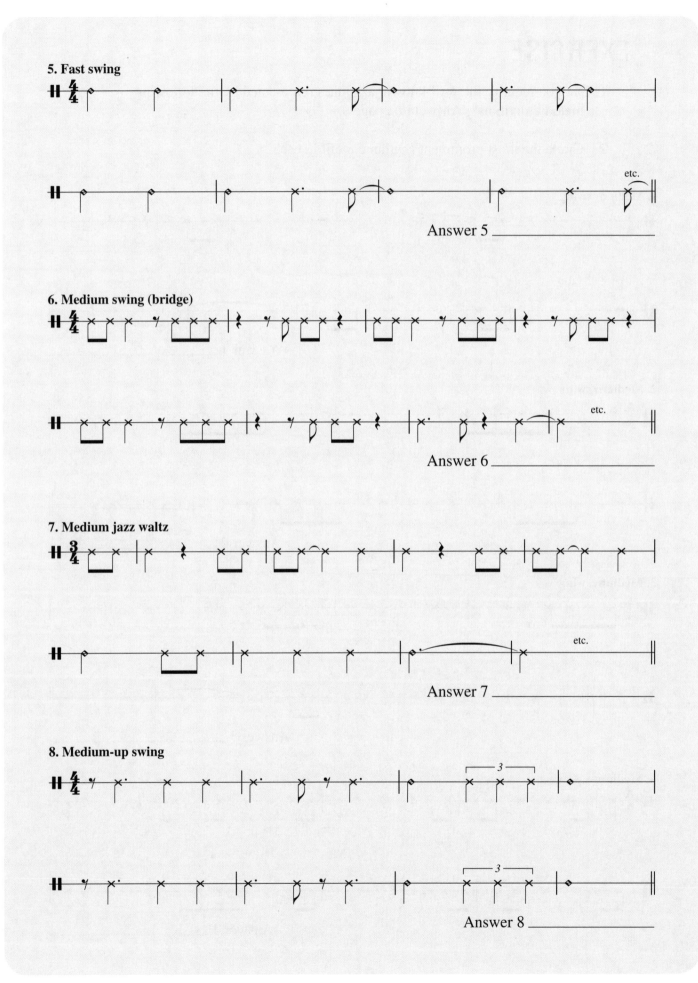

Answer 5 _____

6. Medium swing (bridge)

Answer 6 _____

7. Medium jazz waltz

Answer 7 _____

8. Medium-up swing

Answer 8 _____

9. Medium-up bossa

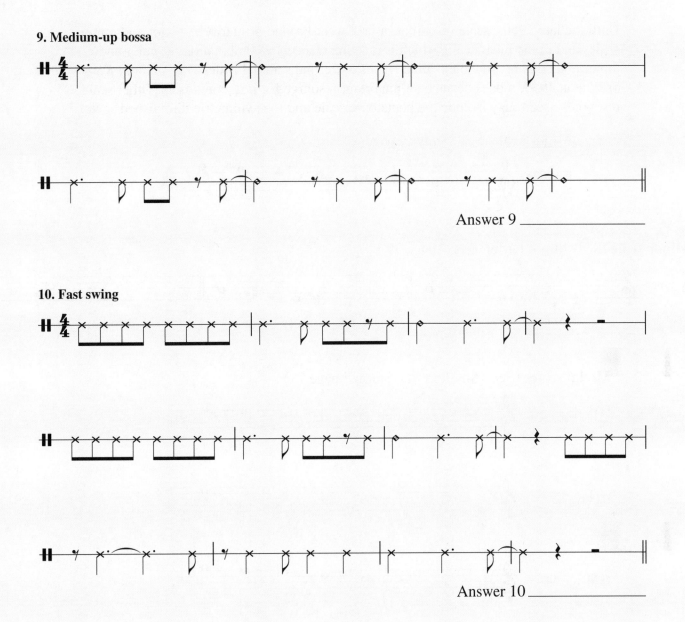

Answer 9 _____

10. Fast swing

Answer 10 _____

Scale Resources

Until the late 1950s, scale resources in jazz were limited primarily to major and minor scales and to the blues scale, which is in some respects a combination of major and minor and contains so-called "blue" notes. After the seminal Miles Davis album *Kind of Blue* in 1959, modes became an important resource for jazz composers. Other scale resources used today include the pentatonic scale and the symmetric diminished scale.

Major scale (See "Strays," page 3.)

Minor scale (See "Minor Differences," page 59.)

Modal scales (See "Any Port in a Storm," page 71)

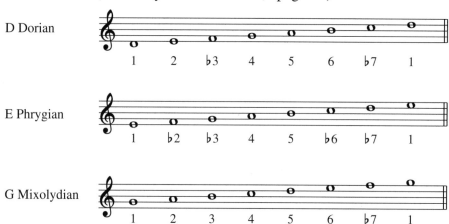

Blues Scale (See "Blues for a Bilious Bystander," page 120.)

Pentatonic scale (See "After Breakfast," page 119.)

Symmetric diminished scale (See "Let's Split," page 122.)

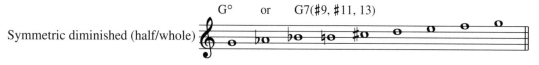

Interval Patterns

A thorough study of melody writing produces certain observations about how composers connect notes together to form melodies. The scales listed above contain an almost unlimited number of potential interval patterns, any of which can be used to create a musical idea at any given moment. Nevertheless, the patterns that most composers use most of the time can be described in general terms in order to help you get started.

First, some definitions:

Step: Melodic movement up or down by a major or minor second (i.e. a whole step or a half step).

Skip: Melodic movement up or down by a major or minor third (i.e. "skipping" over a scale note).

Leap: Melodic movement up or down by a perfect fourth or more.

(Note: Some theory texts define a leap as any interval larger than a major second.)

Most scales are made up of combinations of whole and half steps (see above). Notice, however, that the pentatonic scale contains two minor-third skips. Notice also that the harmonic minor scale contains an augmented second interval between the sixth and seventh step.

Chord arpeggios are made up of a combination of skips, with occasional steps or leaps depending on the chord type and whether an arpeggio happens for more than one octave.

The following interval patterns are common in tonal and modal melody writing, not only in jazz but in most other forms of popular music.

1. **Stepwise motion** is very common. It may be up or down. Stepwise motion usually conforms to the scale of the moment. In some cases, two notes from the scale of the moment may be connected by a chromatic approach.

G major scale

2. **Skips** are common. They may be up or down. They are useful any time you wish to spell a chord melodically. Arpeggiated chords form the basis of many bebop melodies ("up the II, and down the V").

3. **Leaps** are used for dramatic purposes. The wider the leap the more dramatic it is, and the greater the likelihood that it will be followed by a move in the opposite direction.

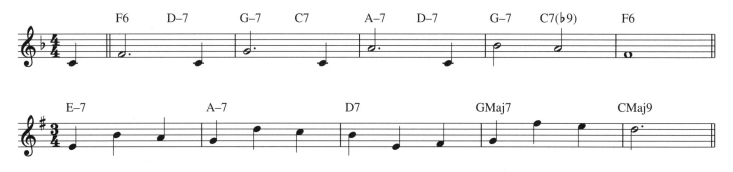

4. **Consecutive leaps** in the same direction should not exceed an octave. The same goes for a leap and a skip in the same direction.

a.

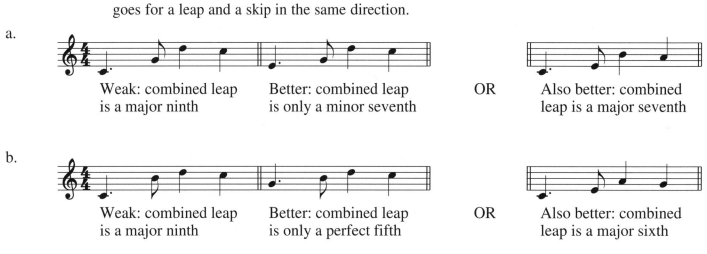

Weak: combined leap is a major ninth

Better: combined leap is only a minor seventh

OR

Also better: combined leap is a major seventh

b.

Weak: combined leap is a major ninth

Better: combined leap is only a perfect fifth

OR

Also better: combined leap is a major sixth

EXERCISE

Using the rhythms given below, write original, diatonic melodies (without chord changes) in the designated scale or mode. Observe the guidelines given previously regarding steps, skips, and leaps when creating your interval patterns.

1. C major

Medium swing

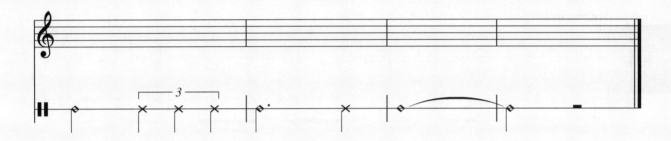

2. C Dorian

Fast swing

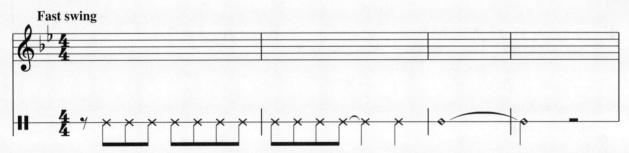

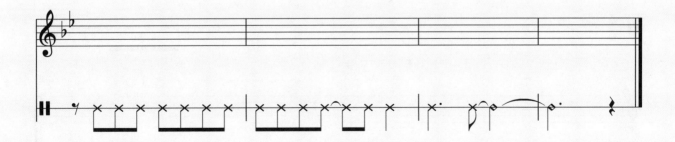

3. F harmonic minor

Medium jazz waltz

4. E Phrygian

Medium fast

5. G Mixolydian

Medium swing

6. C blues scale

Medium swing

7. D minor pentatonic

Fast swing

8. G symmetric diminished

Medium swing

Melodic Variation via Modal Interchange

Modal interchange can be used to create different tonal and modal contexts for a melody. A melody originally conceived in major can be rewritten in minor or in one of the modes. Similarly, a melody originally conceived in minor can be rewritten in major or in one of the modes. And finally, a melody originally conceived in one of the modes can be rewritten in major or in one of the minor modes. These possibilities provide additional options for melodic development in a composition or an arrangement. The examples below demonstrate what happens when this technique is used on Beethoven's "Ode to Joy."

EXERCISE

Rewrite this well-known melody in each of the modes. Play or sing each example for comparison.

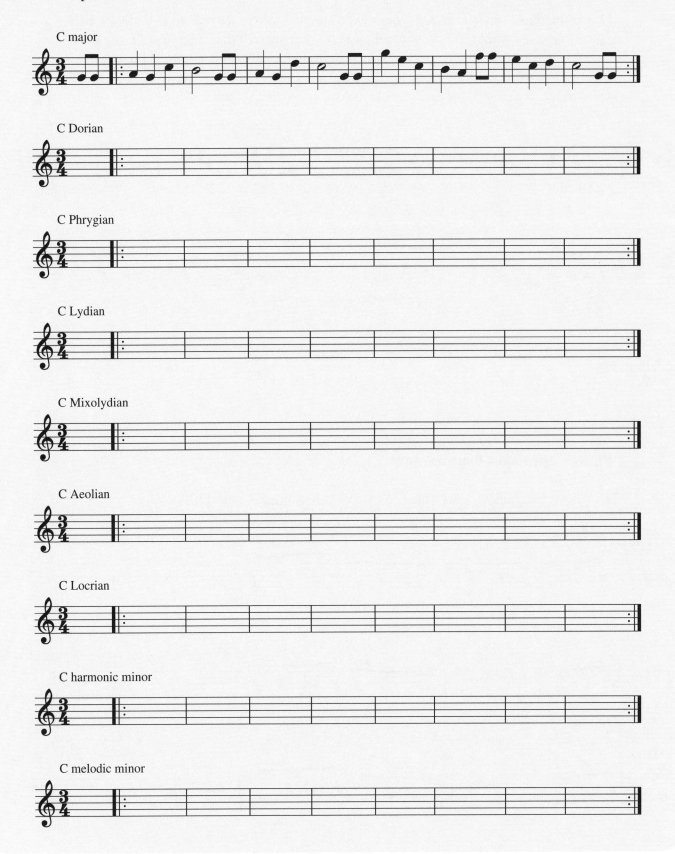

C major

C Dorian

C Phrygian

C Lydian

C Mixolydian

C Aeolian

C Locrian

C harmonic minor

C melodic minor

Melodic Devices and the Rudiments of Form

REPETITION

Motivic repetition

One of the most obvious melodic devices is simple motivic repetition. If you look back at the exercises on pages 7–9, you will observe that each of the examples contains some degree of rhythmic repetition. When rhythmic repetition is combined with pitch repetition, a distinguishing motivic "hook" usually emerges. (See "Strays," page 3, measures 1, 3, 7.)

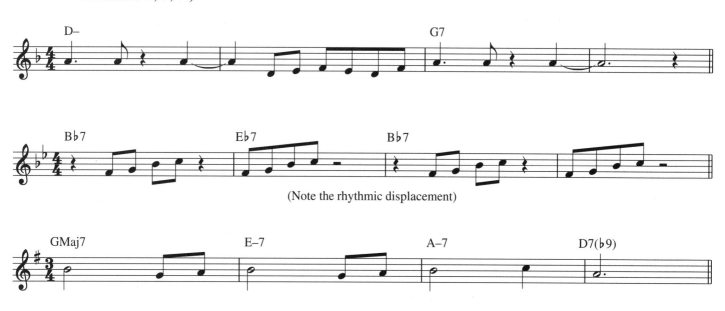

(Note the rhythmic displacement)

Phrase repetition—four measures

This is very common in the blues. (See "After Breakfast," page 119.)

Phrase repetition—eight measures

This is the basis for standard *aaba* and *abac* song form in which the *a* section is repeated in conjunction with other complementary but contrasting phrases. (See "Strays," page 3 for *aaba* form, and "For Bill," page 141 for *abac* form.)

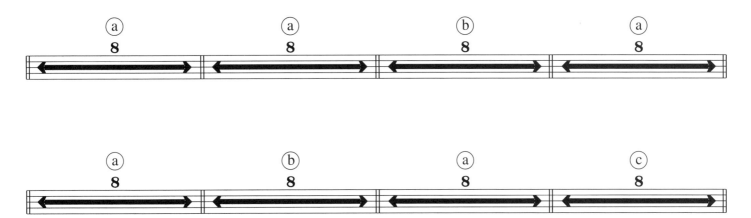

SEQUENCE

A sequence occurs when you transpose a melodic fragment or phrase to a different pitch level. This transposition may be diatonic (in which case the tonality is not disturbed) or exact (in which case a temporary "key-of-the-moment" may suggest itself). The use of sequence takes the concept of repetition to the next level and provides for melodic as well as rhythmic variety.

Motivic sequence

Diatonic

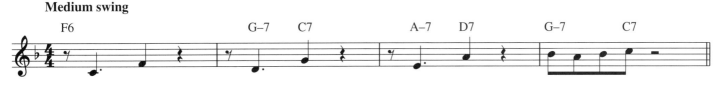

Exact

(See also "Strays," page 3: compare measures 1–2 with 5–6, and 10–11 with 14–15; also measures 16 and 17.)

Two-measure melodic sequence

Note that the chord progression is also sequential. ☐ = interval at which the sequence occurs. (See also "Scrooge," page 147, measures 9–14.)

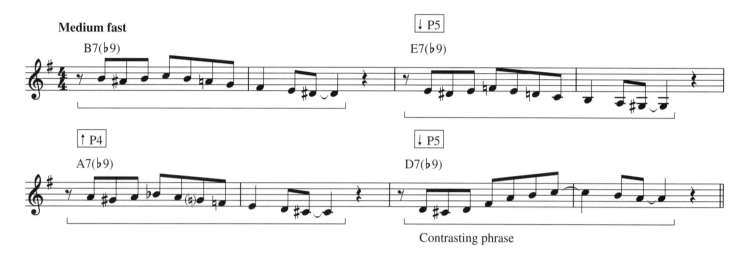

Contrasting phrase

Four-measure melodic sequence

(See also "Scooter," page 128, measures 11–14, 15–18.)

Eight-measure melodic sequence

Examples of this are relatively rare, but check out "Joy Spring" by Clifford Brown and "So What" by Miles Davis.

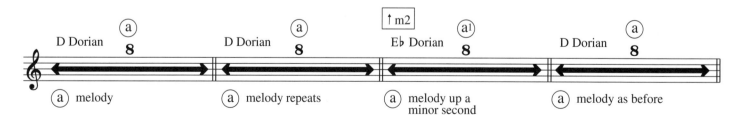

MOTIVIC TRANSFORMATION

Sometimes, too much repetition gets to be monotonous. Motivic transformation is a device that allows you to alter the intervals or the rhythm of a motif in order to prevent the overuse of an idea. You can keep the same rhythm and change the pitches; or you can keep the same pitches and change the rhythm.

Intervallic transformation: Same rhythm, different pitches.

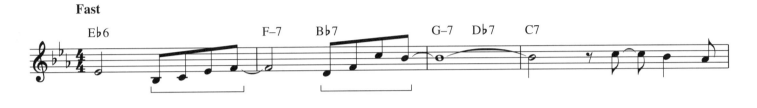

(See also "Samba de Goofed," page 155, measures 17–20 vs. 21–24.)

Rhythmic transformation: Same pitches, different rhythm.

(See also "Samba de Goofed," page 155, measures 1–2 vs. 3–4.)

MOTIVIC EMBELLISHMENT

Motivic embellishment is a device that allows you to activate a simple motif before it becomes too repetitive and monotonous.

(See also "Samba de Goofed," page 155, measure 25 vs. 27.)

EXERCISE

1. (a) Write diatonic sequences to the following two-measure melodic fragment on each degree of the B-flat major scale.

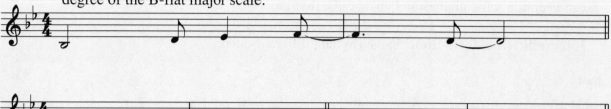

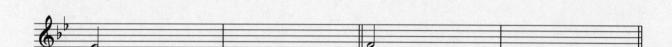

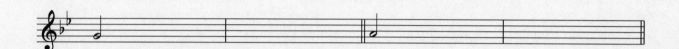

(b) Write exact sequences to the original fragment given above on the given notes written below.

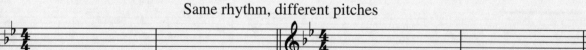

(c) Using the same fragment given in example 1. (a) above, demonstrate motivic transformation.

Same rhythm, different pitches

Same pitches, different rhythms

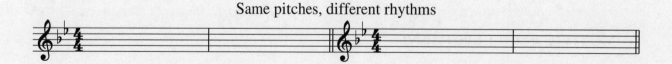

(d) Using the same fragment, demonstrate motivic embellishment.

2. Utilize melodic sequence on the following examples.
   (a) motivic sequence

(b) two-measure melodic sequence (two versions)

(c) four-measure melodic sequence

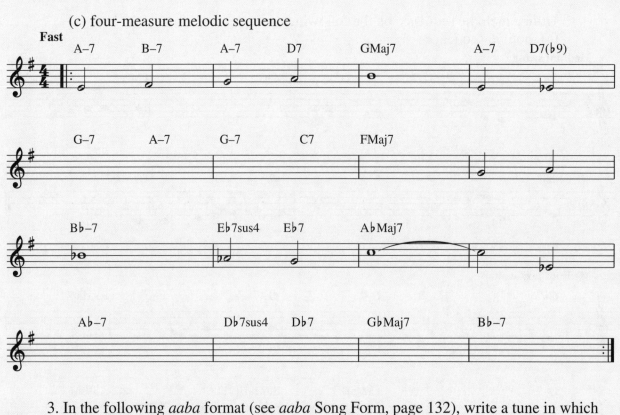

3. In the following *aaba* format (see *aaba* Song Form, page 132), write a tune in which the *a* sections utilize motivic sequence and the *b* section utilizes a two-measure melodic sequence. The principal components are given.

4. In the following *aaba* format, write a tune in which the *a* sections utilize motivic embellishment and the *b* section utilizes motivic transformation. The principal components are given.

MOTIFS BASED ON INTERVALLIC PATTERNS

One method of arriving at intriguing melodic shapes is to work with interval patterns. The following example is based on the interval of the perfect fourth.

In the following example the intervallic pattern is more complex. In the first four measures the motif is a half-step followed by a leap up a perfect fifth, then a leap down a perfect fourth. In the fifth bar that pattern is inverted.

Note: "Soliloquy" is in the key of D-flat major. It is notated here without a key signature so that the intervallic patterns will be as clear as possible.

Soliloquy

Ted Pease

26

EXERCISE

Compose diatonic melodies from the chosen scales based on the given intervallic patterns. Use repetition and sequence freely. (Note: No key signatures are used here, so supply the necessary accidentals in your melodies.)

C Dorian

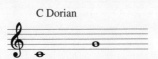

Fast

G Mixolydian

Medium

E♭ Lydian

Slow Latin

MELODIES BASED ON GUIDE TONES

Some of the most enduring melodies ever written have been based on guide tones. For example, "Autumn Leaves" is based on the following guide tone line:

Guide tones are chord tones or tensions that move by step or by common tone to a chord tone or tension in a subsequent chord. They simultaneously imply the chord quality of the moment while creating a need to connect to the next chord in the progression.

Most guide tone lines tend to resolve downward.

However, some of the most dramatic guide tone lines move upward (against the grain).

EXERCISE

The purpose of the following exercise is to find multiple guide tone lines on the same set of chord changes. Voice lead the given guide tones in the designated direction (down or up). Use common tones and/or stepwise motion. Include tensions as appropriate. The same changes are to be used for each eight-measure example.

(Note: alt = altered dominant; ♭9, ♯9, ♭5, ♭13 are all available.)

EMBELLISHING A GUIDE TONE LINE

Effective melodies can be written by simply embellishing a guide tone line. Embellishments consist of passing tones, neighbor tones, escape tones, pickup notes, and suspensions. Anticipations and delayed attacks contribute additional rhythmic interest. (Note: In the following examples, embellishments are circled.)

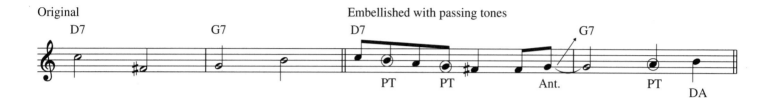

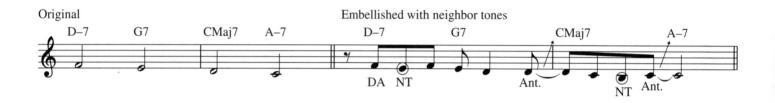

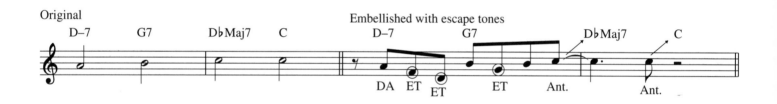

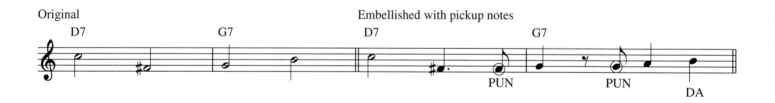

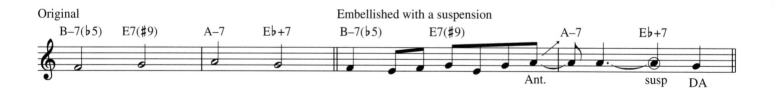

See "And Why Not?" on the next page.

And Why Not?

Ted Pease

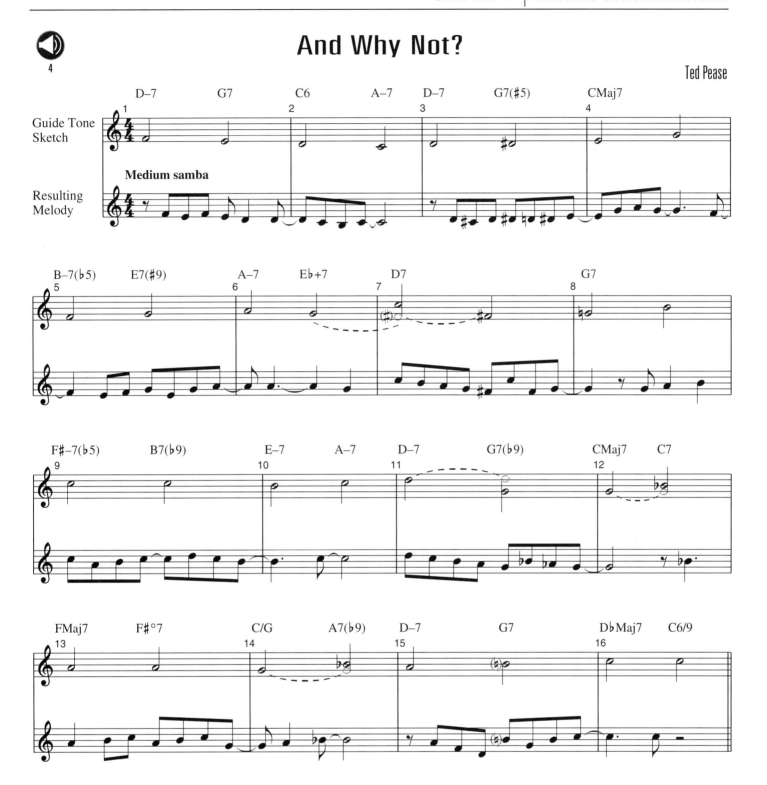

As you observe this example, notice that:

1. Guide tones can move up (measures 3–5, 10–11, and 15–16), down (measures 1–2, 9–10, 13–14), and sideways (measures 9, 13, and 16).

2. Within the duration of a chord, you can skip or leap to another guide tone before moving on (measures 4, 7, and 8).

3. You can also skip or leap when two chords share guide tones (measures 11, 12, and 14).

EXERCISE

1. Write an eight-measure melody that consists of an embellished version of the given guide tone sketch. Label your embellishments.

Sketch

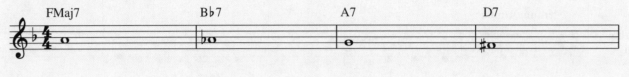

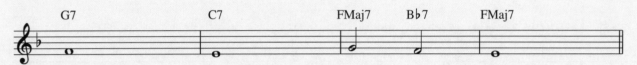

Your Melody

2. Write an eight-measure melody that consists of an embellished version of the given guide tone sketch. Label your embellishments.

Sketch

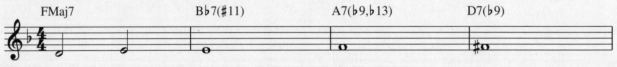

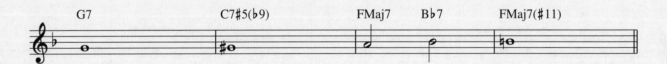

Your Melody

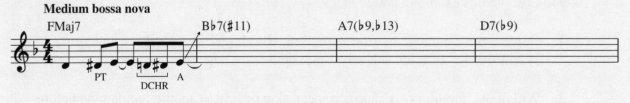

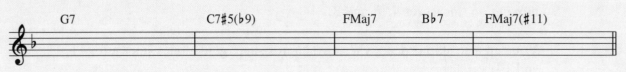

3. Create your own guide tone sketch on the given changes. Then write a melody that
   consists of an embellished version of the sketch. Label your embellishments.

Sketch

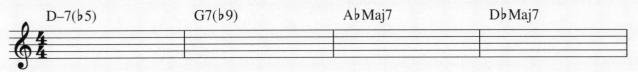

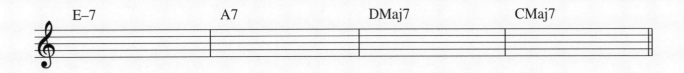

Your Melody

Ballad

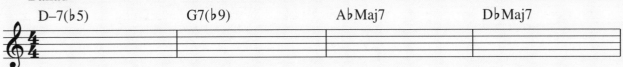

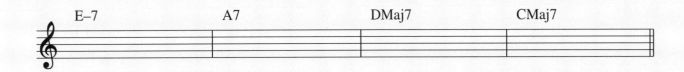

MELODIES BASED ON COMPOUND LINES

Some melodies are based on compound lines. Compound lines consist of two (or more) guide tone lines that proceed through a set of chord changes simultaneously. A melody can be created by alternating between the guide tones. Observe the example below, and then turn to the tune "Diminishing Returns" on the next page.

meas. 1–8

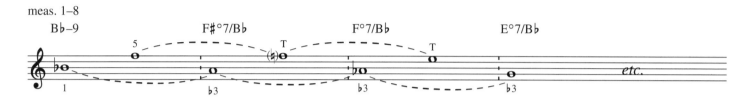

meas. 21–27

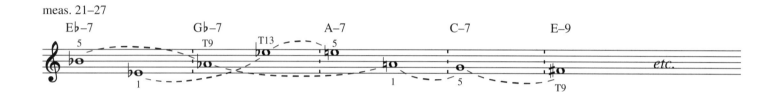

meas. 29–46

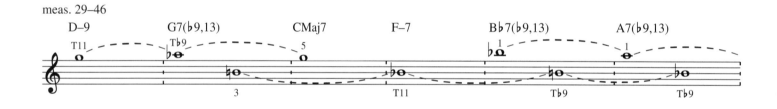

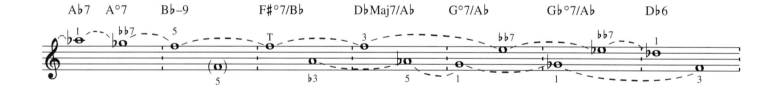

Diminishing Returns

Ted Pease

EXERCISES

Complete a compound line on the given changes. Then write a melody that consists of an embellished version of the sketch. Label your embellishments.

ANTECEDENT AND CONSEQUENT PHRASES

Antecedent and consequent phrases are complementary musical ideas that, when combined in longer phrases, produce both variety and balance. In effect, they help produce a musical conversation similar to language, as in:

Antecedent: "Who won the ball game last night?"

Consequent: "The Red Sox won 3 to 2."

or, as in a one-sided monologue:

Antecedent: "Did you hear the latest?"

Consequent: "I'm being audited by the IRS!"

Most jazz melodies rely on symmetrical phrase structure. This promotes balance. Therefore, antecedent and consequent phrases are usually the same length. (When they are not, you will likely hear vigorous and careful discussion among musicians at rehearsals!)

Most antecedent and consequent phrases are four measures long, as in the example below:

(See "Your Smile," page 135.)

Sometimes, antecedent and consequent phrases are eight measures long:

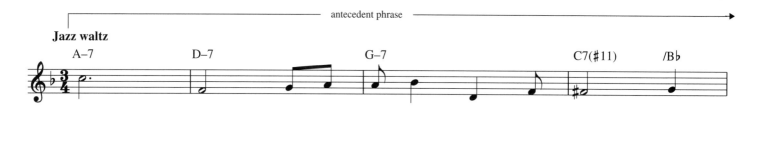

(See "For Bill," page 141.)

Asymmetric phrase structuring is less common. Care must be taken to avoid incoherence. The following example has a four-measure antecedent phrase and a six-measure consequent phrase. Notice how the ear tries to make the example symmetrical by subdividing the consequent phrase into two measures plus four measures, thereby breaking up the total of ten measures into four/two/four.

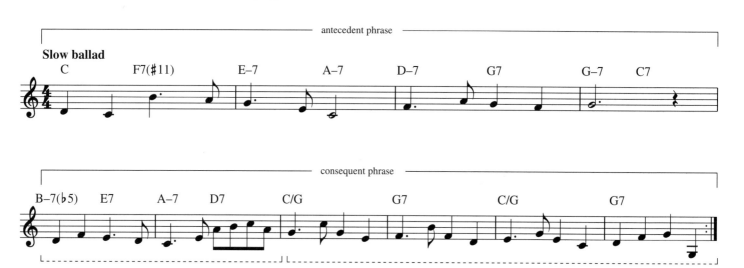

It is very important to create a sense of balance between antecedent and consequent phrases. Otherwise, you may create a musical "non sequitur" (Latin for "does not follow"). The examples below demonstrate this unfortunate effect.

Problems:
1. Consequent phrase sounds like the beginning of a different tune.
2. Drastic contrast in rhythmic velocity and density.

Problems:
1. Simple diatonic melody in bossa nova style (measures 1–4) is interrupted by bebop lick in measure 5.
2. Radical tonal departure from G major in the consequent phrase.
3. Awkward harmonic rhythm in measures 6–8.

To avoid musical non sequiturs:
1. Make sure your consequent phrase reflects the melodic rhythm of the antecedent phrase.
2. Avoid abrupt changes in melodic density and contour between phrases.
3. Maintain a consistent harmonic style.
4. Avoid drastic differences in melodic range between phrases.

EXERCISES

Write consequent phrases to the following antecedent phrases.

Using *aaba* song form, supply consequent phrases for the given antecedent phrases in the *a* section and in the bridge.

PITCH CONTOUR AND RANGE

Pitch contour plays a definite role in melody writing. The effect of a smooth line within a narrow range tends to be relaxing, whereas a rough or jagged line that covers a wide range tends to be more intense. The following examples are drawn from two tunes with very different pitch contours.

(See "Any Friday," page 120.)

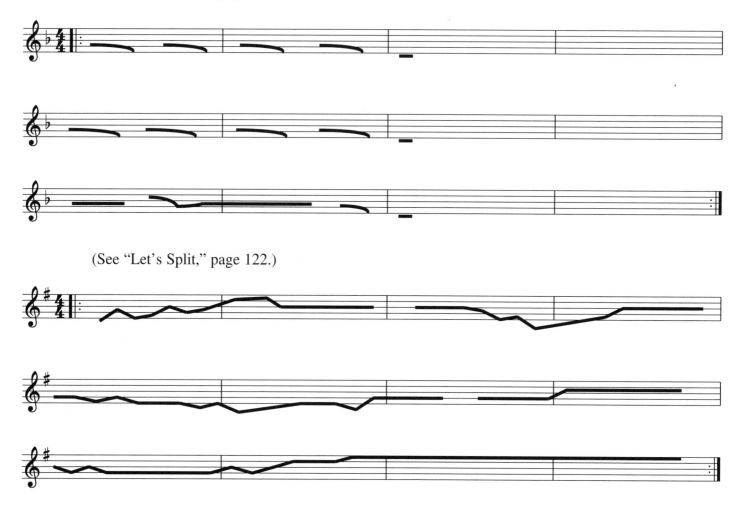

(See "Let's Split," page 122.)

APEX (CLIMAX)

Most jazz tunes have an apex. The apex (or climax) is the highest note in the tune. It is strategically placed to provide the most dramatic moment and usually (but definitely not always) occurs about two-thirds to three-quarters of the way through.

Look through the book at the various tunes and place a check mark over the highest note in each. Compare measure numbers to determine whether the apex is early or late. Here is a short list of some of the tunes, along with a measure count for the apex and the total number of measures.

"Samba de Goofed," page 155; apex in measure 15 out of 40 (early)
"Scrooge," page 147; apex in measure 21 out of 32 (average)
"Sez Who?" page 144; apex in measure 21 out of 24 (late)

EXERCISES

1. Write a sixteen-measure melody that stays smoothly within the following range.

2. Write a sixteen-measure melody that encompasses the following range and contains the apex in measure 11.

MELODIC TENSION AS A FUNCTION OF STYLE

Tensions were a relatively uncommon melodic choice for jazz composers during the 1920s and 1930s. Most melodies were based on chord arpeggios or scale patterns that did not expose these relatively dissonant notes. Those tensions that were used usually resolved immediately to related chord tones a step away in the manner of a suspension or an appoggiatura, or they were treated as approach notes.

Since the advent of bebop in the mid-1940s, melodic tensions have played an increasingly important role in jazz performance and composition. Today, unresolved tensions are part of the musical palette available to all writers.

Older Styles

Low tension level

Medium swing

(See "Scooter," page 128.)

Newer Styles

Higher tension level

Bossa nova

(See "Let's Split," page 122.)

EXERCISES

Construct a sixteen-measure melody outline in half notes. As a challenge, limit yourself to melodic tensions on each chord. Try to organize the tensions into intervallic patterns, or use them as guide tones and voice lead them. Have the apex in the twelfth measure. (Major 7 may be considered a tension in this exercise.)

Now create a melody by embellishing your melody outline. Use four-measure antecedent and consequent phrases.

Source Material — Melodic Considerations

SCALE RESOURCES

1. Major scale
>See "Strays," page 3.
>The Beauty of All Things (Laurence Hobgood/Kurt Elling)
>A Child Is Born (Thad Jones)
>Honeysuckle Rose ("Fats" Waller)
>It's Only Music (Gary Willis)
>Moment's Notice (John Coltrane)
>Perdido (Juan Tizol)
>Yesterday and Today (Dario Eskenazi)

2. Minor scales
>See "Minor Differences," page 59.
>Django (John Lewis)
>How Insensitive (Antonio Carlos Jobim)
>Keep It Moving (Wynton Kelly)
>Song for My Father (Horace Silver)

3. Modal scales
>See "Any Port in a Storm," page 71.
>Don't Let It Go (Vincent Herring): Lydian
>Impressions (John Coltrane): Dorian
>Jeannine (Duke Pearson): Dorian
>La Fiesta (Chick Corea): Spanish Phrygian
>Little Sunflower (Freddie Hubbard): Dorian
>Passion Dance (McCoy Tyner): Mixolydian
>Pursuance (John Coltrane): Aeolian
>Tell Me a Bedtime Story (Herbie Hancock): Lydian

4. Blues scale
>See "Blues for a Bilious Bystander," page 120.
>Birdland (Joe Zawinul)
>Filthy McNasty (Horace Silver)
>Loco Motiv (Larry Gales)

5. Pentatonic scale
>See "After Breakfast," page 119.
>Pursuance (John Coltrane)
>Sonny Moon for Two (Sonny Rollins)

6. Symmetric diminished scale
>See "Let's Split," page 122.
>Killer Joe (Benny Golson): bridge

MELODIC VARIATION VIA MODAL INTERCHANGE

>All Blues (Miles Davis): G Mixolydian to G Dorian
>No More Blues (Antonio Carlos Jobim): D minor to D major

MELODIC REPETITION

1. Motivic Repetition
    See "Strays," page 3.
    A Child Is Born (Thad Jones)
    Blue Monk (Thelonious Monk)
    Four (Miles Davis)
    I Mean You (Thelonious Monk)
    In a Mellow Tone (Duke Ellington)
    Killer Joe (Benny Golson)
    Passion Dance (McCoy Tyner)
    Perdido (Juan Tizol)
    So What (Miles Davis)
    Straight No Chaser (Thelonious Monk)

2. Four-Measure Phrase Repetition
    See "After Breakfast," page 119.
    Jeannine (Duke Pearson)
    Naima (John Coltrane)
    Pent Up House (Sonny Rollins)
    Rosewood (Woody Shaw)
    Sonny Moon for Two (Sonny Rollins)
    St. Thomas (Sonny Rollins)

3. Eight-Measure Phrase Repetition
    See "Your Smile," page 135.
    Afternoon in Paris (John Lewis)
    Black Nile (Wayne Shorter)
    I Remember Clifford (Benny Golson)
    Maiden Voyage (Herbie Hancock)
    Satin Doll (Duke Ellington)

MELODIC SEQUENCE

1. Motivic Sequence
    See "Strays," page 3.
    Cute (Neal Hefti): diatonic (measures 9–12)
    Well You Needn't (Thelonious Monk): exact (bridge)

2. Two-Measure Melodic Sequence
    See "Scrooge" page 147 (measures 9–14).
    Afternoon in Paris (John Lewis): exact (measures 1–4)
    Airegin (Sonny Rollins): exact (measures 9–20)
    Satin Doll (Duke Ellington): diatonic (measures 1–4)
    Shiny Stockings (Frank Foster): exact (measures 9–14)
    Woody'n You (Dizzy Gillespie): exact (measures 1–6)

3. Four-Measure Melodic Sequence

See the bridge of "Scooter," page 128.
Airegin (Sonny Rollins): exact (measures 1–8)
Blue Bossa (Kenny Dorham): diatonic (measures 1–8)
Loco Motiv (Larry Gales): exact (bridge)
New Girl (Duke Pearson): exact (measures 1–8)
Satin Doll (Duke Ellington): exact (bridge)
Woody'n You (Dizzy Gillespie): exact (bridge)

4. Eight-Measure Melodic Sequence

Black Narcissus (Joe Henderson): exact (measures 1–16)
Joy Spring (Clifford Brown): exact (measures 1–16)
So What (Miles Davis): exact (bridge)

MOTIVIC TRANSFORMATION

1. Same Rhythm, Different Pitches

See "Samba de Goofed," page 155.
Ana Maria (Wayne Shorter)
Maiden Voyage (Herbie Hancock)
The Midnight Sun Will Never Set (Quincy Jones)

2. Same Pitches, Different Rhythm

See "Samba de Goofed," page 155.
Spain (Chick Corea): Compare the last part of A with the last part of C.
Blues for a Bilious Bystander (Ted Pease): See page 120.

MOTIVIC EMBELLISHMENT

See "Samba de Goofed," page 155.
Along Came Betty (Benny Golson): measures 1–4
Ecaroh (Horace Silver): A section
Memory and Desire (Billy Childs): measures 1–10
Nica's Dream (Horace Silver): measures 1–8

MOTIFS BASED ON INTERVALLIC PATTERNS

See "Soliloquy," page 26.
E.S.P. (Wayne Shorter): fourths
Giant Steps (John Coltrane): thirds
In Walked Bud (Thelonious Monk): expanding intervals
Misterioso (Thelonious Monk): sixths
Pent Up House (Sonny Rollins): mixed intervals
Witch Hunt (Wayne Shorter): fourths

MELODIES BASED ON GUIDE TONES

See "And Why Not?" page 31.
Ceora (Lee Morgan)
Dolphin Dance (Herbie Hancock)
How Insensitive (Antonio Carlos Jobim)

MELODIES BASED ON COMPOUND LINES

See "Diminishing Returns," page 35.
I'll Remember August (Ralph Towner)
In Walked Bud (Thelonious Monk)
Jordu (Duke Jordan)

ANTECEDENT AND CONSEQUENT PHRASES

1. Four-measure phrases
See "Your Smile," page 135.
Anthropology (Charlie Parker)
Bernie's Tune (Bernie Miller)
Come Sunday (Duke Ellington)
I Remember Clifford (Benny Golson)
Keep It Moving (Wynton Kelly)
Morning (Clare Fischer)
Take the A Train (Billy Strayhorn)

2. Eight-measure phrases
See "For Bill," page 141.
Ceora (Lee Morgan)
Epiphany (Denny Zeitlin)
Jeannine (Duke Pearson)
Moment's Notice (John Coltrane)
Mr. Softee (Alan Pasqua)
Nica's Dream (Horace Silver)
Pensativa (Clare Fischer)
Shiny Stockings (Frank Foster)
Yesterday and Today (Dario Eskenazi)

3. Asymmetric phrases
See "Diminishing Returns," page 35.
The Beauty of All Things (Laurence Hobgood/Kurt Elling)
Infant Eyes (Wayne Shorter)
New Girl (Duke Pearson)
Stablemates (Benny Golson)

PITCH CONTOUR AND RANGE

1. Smooth
See "Any Friday," page 120.
Gregory Is Here (Horace Silver)
In a Mellow Tone (Duke Ellington)
Moment's Notice (John Coltrane)

2. Rough
See "Thad's Pad," page 129.
Inner Urge (Joe Henderson)
Isotope (Joe Henderson)
Memory and Desire (Billy Childs)
Upper Manhattan Medical Group (Billy Strayhorn)

APEX (CLIMAX)

See "Scrooge," page 147.
Along Came Betty (Benny Golson): measure 29
Ceora (Lee Morgan): measure 28
Shiny Stockings (Frank Foster): measure 29

MELODIC TENSION AS A FUNCTION OF STYLE

See "Let's Split," page 122.
Epiphany (Denny Zeitlin)
The Everlasting Night (Gary Willis)
Ladybird (Tadd Dameron)
Stablemates (Benny Golson)
Time Remembered (Bill Evans)

CHAPTER 2
Harmonic Considerations

Jazz harmony is mostly tonal or modal. Composers such as Charles Mingus and Cecil Taylor have experimented with atonal techniques, and so-called "free jazz" sometimes assumes an atonal quality. Nevertheless, most jazz composers have retained a relatively conservative approach to harmony (compared to classical composers such as Stravinsky, Bartók, or Alban Berg!), and the harmonic language they use is, in most cases, recognizable.

This is not to say that jazz harmony is limited or uninteresting. Part of the challenge of playing and writing good jazz is to use conventional chord changes, reharmonizations, modulations, and voicings in unique and surprising ways. Furthermore, part of the basic charm of jazz is that its harmonic language is so well understood by experienced players that total strangers can perform together at a moment's notice.

One must understand the difference between jazz harmony and jazz voicings. Jazz harmony deals with the progression of chords in time (the "changes") and the possible harmonic substitutions that might be made for more familiar patterns. Jazz voicings are the individual harmonic sounds that composers, arrangers, and performers produce when providing vertical structures within a progression. These structures may be open or closed, clear or ambiguous, and percussive or sustained depending on the situation. The relationship between voicings and changes provides much of the harmonic interest in jazz.

Until the mid-1950s, most jazz compositions were tonal. It could be said that a particular piece was in this major key or that minor key. Jazz voicings consisted of seventh chords and their extensions (ninths, elevenths, and thirteenths) and were built up from the root in thirds ("tertian" harmony). Functional harmony was the prevailing harmonic system of analysis. (Functional harmony recognizes the preeminence of tonic, subdominant, and dominant chords and their common-tone substitutes in virtually every style of classical and popular music.) All of these predictable characteristics produced a level of comfort among jazz musicians, who welcomed the commonality of the musical language. (A discussion of tonal harmony in major and minor keys begins on page 52.)

In the late 1950s, jazz composers such as George Russell and Miles Davis began using modes in their compositions. George Russell used various scales and modes in polytonal and polymodal relationships in compositions such as "All About Rosie." Miles Davis turned the jazz world upside down in his seminal album *Kind of Blue* with modal compositions such as "So What" and "All Blues." The latter two classic jazz compositions were also noteworthy for their extended harmonic rhythms and for the use of ostinatos. They sounded quite different from the bebop and hard bop tunes that were also being written at the time. (A discussion of modal harmony begins on page 62.)

Pianist Bill Evans, who performed with George Russell and Miles Davis on the aforementioned recordings, contributed to the impact of the new modal approach by voicing chords in fourths and in seconds, as well as in thirds. These new voicings were unfamiliar to most jazz musicians at first, but their usage was eagerly adopted in the early 1960s by such pianists as McCoy Tyner and Herbie Hancock, and by such composer/arrangers as Oliver Nelson and Thad Jones. By the mid 1960s this new harmonic language had been absorbed and was being used along with the earlier styles by most composers and players of the day.

Some tunes of the 1960s also strayed farther and farther away from functional harmony as deliberate tonal identity became less important. Chromatic harmony and parallel harmony (so-called "constant structures") became more and more common. The chord progressions of Wayne Shorter (e.g., "Nefertiti") and Herbie Hancock (e.g., "Maiden Voyage") were sometimes purposefully ambiguous. The I chord was no longer a frequent target point, and consequently the tonality was often vague. Sometimes it seemed as if any chord could follow any other chord, melody permitting. (Chromatic harmony is discussed on page 80. Constant structures are discussed on page 92.)

In the 1970s and 1980s, fusion (see page 185) helped to further focus the attention of composers, arrangers, and performers on the role of the bass. Inasmuch as the electric bass was more like a bass guitar than an upright bass, and because it was amplified, virtuoso electric bass players such as Jaco Pastorius and Stanley Clarke were able to bring bass lines to the textural foreground not only in solos but also in accompaniments. Harmonies that further emphasized the bass, such as chordal inversions and "slash" chords (see page 90), became more and more common.

In recent years, composers such as John Scofield have occasionally employed ostinatos and other bass lines that suggest a polytonal relationship (or at least a disconnect) with the melody. Such Scofield tunes as "Stranger to the Light" and "I Can See Your House from Here" are good examples.

Contemporary jazz harmony presents a virtual kaleidoscope of sounds ranging from simple triads to complex polychords. Aspiring jazz composers need to have a firm grasp of all its aspects.

Tonal Harmony (Major Key Orientation)

In tonal harmony, the **I** chord of a piece is at the center of the harmonic universe. The **I** chord exhibits the most gravity, and all other chords that are used in a piece have a role in progressing to or from it. Primary dominant resolution (**V7/I**) and primary subdominant resolution (**IV/I**) and their respective derivatives are the most common progressions.

Since many jazz voicings are based on seventh chords and their available tensions, it is helpful to know that the other diatonic seventh chords in major (II–7, III–7, VI–7, and VII–7(♭5)) provide common-tone derivatives ("aliases") and substitutions for the tonic chord, the subdominant chord, and the dominant chord. Because of their respective common tones, III–7 and VI–7 are similar to the **I** chord and often have tonic function; II–7 is similar to the **IV** chord and often has subdominant function. VII–7(♭5) is similar to the **V** chord because it contains the tritone. It can have a somewhat weak dominant function when progressing to **I** major (e.g., B–7(♭5) to CMaj7), or subdominant minor function when progressing to V7/I minor in the relative minor (e.g., B–7(♭5) to E7(♭9) to A–).

Secondary dominant progressions (**V7/II–7, V7/III–7, V7/IV, V7/V, V7/VI–7, V7/VII–7(♭5)**) create a secondary level of harmonic gravity. In addition, each of these **V7** chords has a substitute dominant available to take its place at the whim of the performer or composer/arranger. The substitute dominant contains the same tritone as the "real" dominant and acts as an alias for it. The root of a substitute dominant chord is an augmented fourth (or its equivalent, the diminished fifth) away from the root of the "real" dominant chord (e.g. D♭7 is the substitute dominant for G7 in the key of C major. Conversely, G7 is the substitute dominant for D♭7 in the key of G♭ major.) Dominant resolution produces root motion down a perfect fifth to the target chord. Substitute dominant resolution produces root motion down a half step to the target chord.

Passing diminished chords move up by half step between I and II–7, between II–7 and III–7, between IVMaj7 and V7, and between V7 and VI–7. They mimic secondary dominants because of the common tones that are shared.

Traditional practice in jazz harmony allows the placement of the related II–7 chord before any dominant seventh chord. The related II–7 chord comes from the same "key of the moment" as the V7. Therefore D–7 is the related II–7 of G7 regardless of where it occurs in a progression. E♭–7 is the related II–7 of A♭7, F♯-7 is the related II–7 of B7, and so on. Related II–7 chords are often used before substitute dominants as well.

The following chart summarizes the above in the key of C major. The tune "Catch Me If You Can" on the following page utilizes a variety of tonal progressions.

Harmonic Universe in C Major

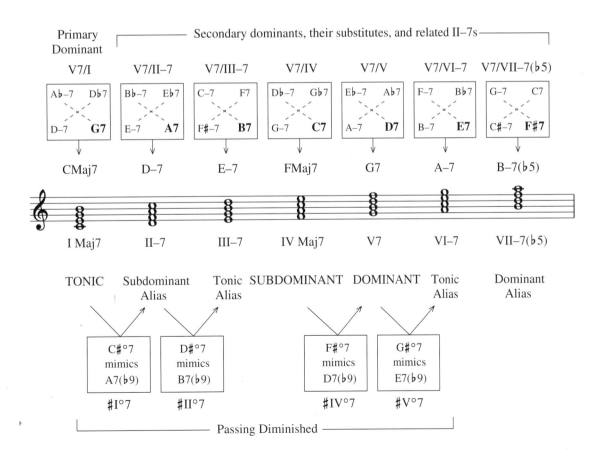

Catch Me If You Can

Ted Pease

Measures 1–8 demonstrate the following secondary dominants: V7/II, V7/III, V7/IV, V7/V, and V7/VI. Measures 9–16 demonstrate the following passing diminished chords, which mimic the designated secondary dominants: #I°7 (mimics V7/II), #II°7 (mimics V7/III), #IV°7 (mimics V7/V), and #V°7 (mimics V7/VI). Measures 17–20 demonstrate a two-measure melodic and harmonic sequence. Measures 21–24 demonstrate a sequence of II/Vs in four different keys of the moment: C, E, A♭, G♭. Measures 25 and 26 demonstrate passing diminished chords again. Measures 27–32 demonstrate more secondary dominants.

EXERCISES

Complete the following charts.

Harmonic Universe in F Major

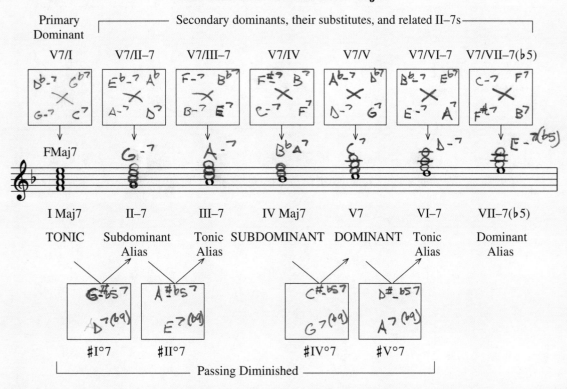

Harmonic Universe in B♭ Major

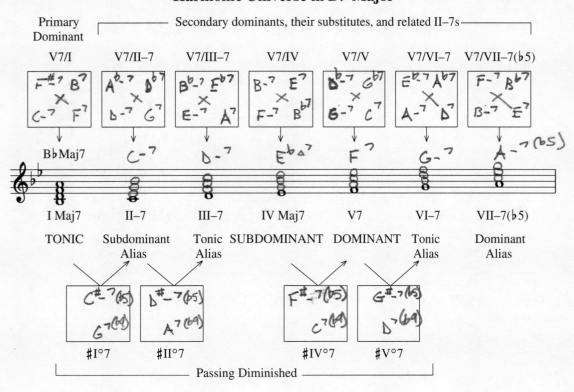

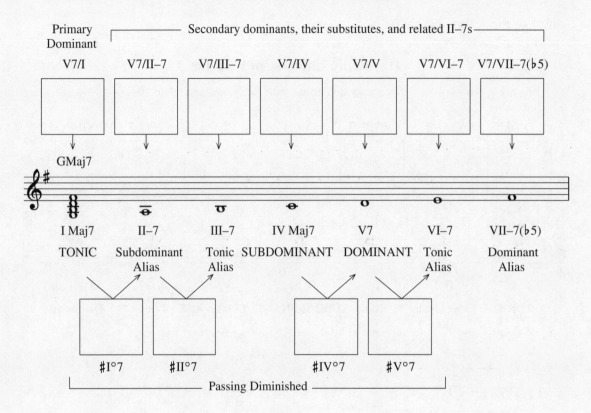

Harmonic Universe in G Major

Supply the missing item in the following musical equations. Assume that these are tonal situations in various major keys. The first two are given.

1. B♭ major: V7 = F7

2. C major: V7/II–7 = A7

3. F major: V7/V = G7

4. D♭ major: V7/IV = D♭7

5. B♭ major: V7/VI–7 = D7

6. E♭ major: # I°7 = E°7

7. A♭ major: V7/II = F7

8. G major: # II°7 = A#°7

9. E♭ major: V7/IV = E♭7

10. C major: subV7/II–7 = E♭

11. D♭ major: sub V7/IV = ____

12. F major: _____ = A♭7

13. G♭ major: _____ = D♭7

14. _____: subV7/V = E♭7

15. C major: related II–7 of V7/IV = ____

16. E♭ major: related II–7 of sub V7/II–7 = ____

17. _____: related II–7 of V7/V = D–7

18. A♭ major: related II–7 of _____ = E♭–7

19. B♭ major: related II–7 of sub V7/II–7 = ____

20. C major: ____ = F#°7

56

Tonal Harmony (Minor Key Orientation)

There are three forms of the minor scale: natural minor, melodic minor, and harmonic minor. Natural minor contains a diatonic sixth and seventh degree. Melodic minor contains a raised sixth and seventh degree, while harmonic minor contains the diatonic sixth degree and a raised seventh degree.

The following charts demonstrate (respectively) the harmonic universe of C natural minor, C harmonic minor, and C melodic minor, and they show the diatonic seventh chords that are produced on each note of these respective C minor scales.

Harmonic Universe in C Natural Minor

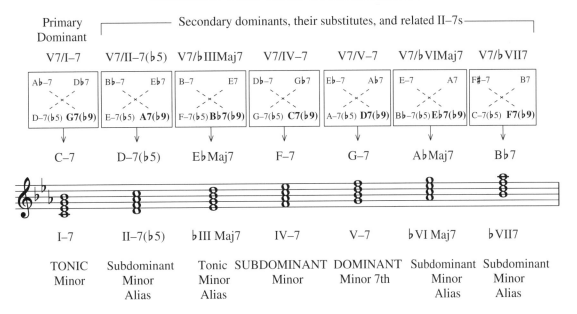

Harmonic Universe in C Harmonic Minor

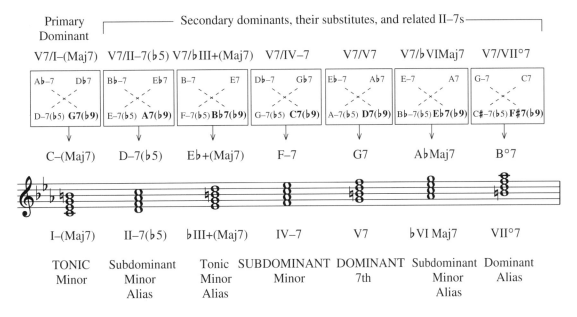

Note: Primary and secondary dominant chords in a minor key tend to use ♭9 as a harmonic tension because it has a darker sound than ♮9. When ♭9 is used, the related II–7 chord usually takes ♭5, because ♭5 and ♭9 of the dominant are the same pitch. The substitute dominants take ♮9, and their related II–7s take ♮5.

Harmonic Universe in C Melodic Minor

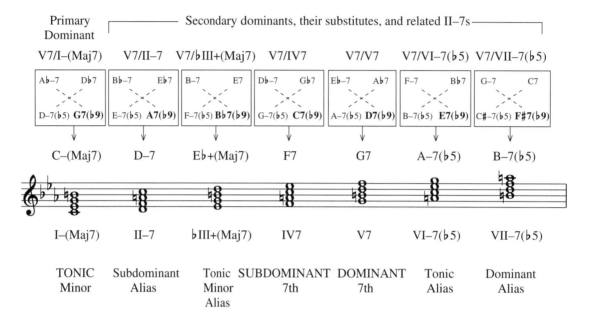

The three forms of the minor scale are interchangeable, and you may notice that some tunes contain references to all three depending on the whim of the composer. In the following example, "Minor Differences," you will find all three forms of the A minor scale being used. For reference, these scales are shown on the second staff (below the melody). Notice that some of them are built up from the root of the chord-of-the-moment, thereby indicating the correct chord scale for that chord (i.e., the mode of the designated minor scale).

Note: For a thorough discussion of chord-scale theory see *Modern Jazz Voicings* by Ted Pease and Ken Pullig.

Minor Differences

Ted Pease

"A harmonic minor (5–5)" supplies the correct chord scale for E7(♭9). This is the A harmonic minor scale shown in its "5–5" mode:

EXERCISES

Complete the following charts:

Harmonic Universe in D Natural Minor

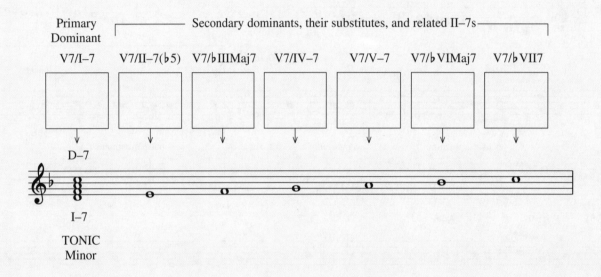

Harmonic Universe in G Harmonic Minor

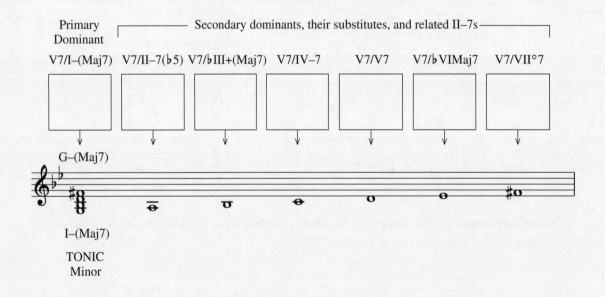

Harmonic Universe in A Melodic Minor

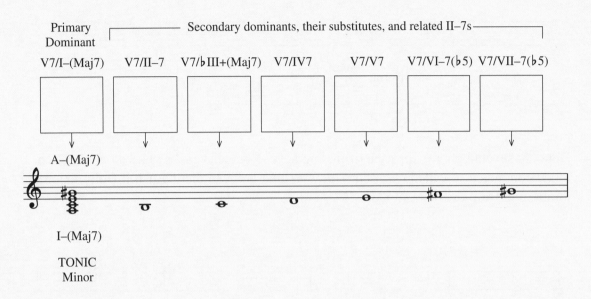

Supply the missing item in each equation. Assume that these are tonal situations in various minor keys. For the sake of consistency, use ♭5 and (♭9) on II—7 and V7 chords respectively. The first two are given.

1. A harmonic minor: V7(♭9) = E7(♭9)

2. G natural minor: II–7(♭5)= A–7(♭5)

3. C harmonic minor: V7/II–7(♭5) = _____

4. F natural minor: _____ = C–7

5. _____: V7(♭9) = F7(♭9)

6. _____: V7(♭9)/IV7 = C7(♭9)

7. E harmonic minor: F♯–7(♭5) = _____

8. D melodic minor: _____ = V7(♭9)

9. C melodic minor: subV7/II–7 = _____

10. F harmonic minor: subV7/V7 = _____

11. D harmonic minor: _____ = B♭7

12. A melodic minor: _____ = B♭7

13. _____: II—7(♭5) = F–7(♭5)

14. _____: related II–7(♭5) of V7(♭9)/VI–7(♭5) = B–7(♭5)

15. E melodic minor: _____ = II–7

Modal Harmony

The modes have provided fertile musical soil for jazz composers since the late 1950s. In effect, modes can be viewed as displacements of the major scale.

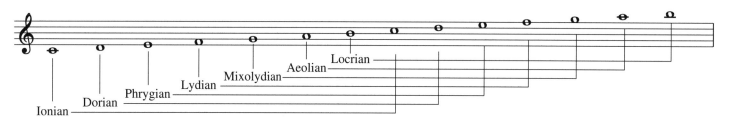

Diatonic seventh chords for each of the modes can be derived, as shown below. Each mode contains a so-called *characteristic note* that helps to distinguish it from major and minor, and from the other modes.

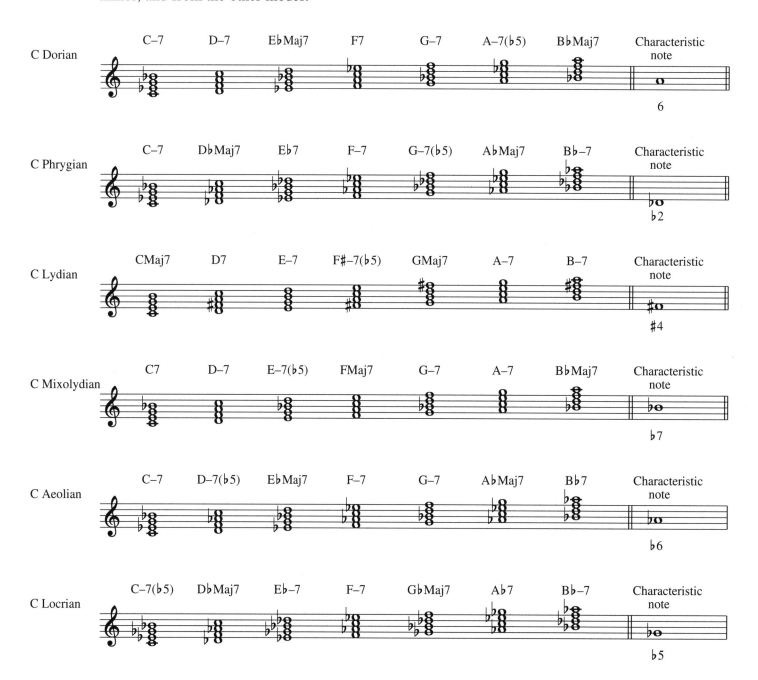

Most textbook explanations of modal harmony warn you to beware of the diatonic tritone in each mode, lest it pull you into the relative major key. This warning is valuable, but it can be somewhat limiting, especially in jazz composition. Since the characteristic note of each mode is also a note in the diatonic tritone of that mode, it stands to reason that the tritone may actually have a role in helping to establish the sound of that mode.

Play the examples below on the piano and you will see and hear that these voicings, as simple as they are, are potential **I** chords in D Dorian, E Phrygian, F Lydian, G Mixolydian, A Aeolian, and B Locrian respectively. Note that the respective tritones are given strong support from each modal tonic in the bass clef. This helps anchor the tritone and ensures modal rather than tonal orientation.

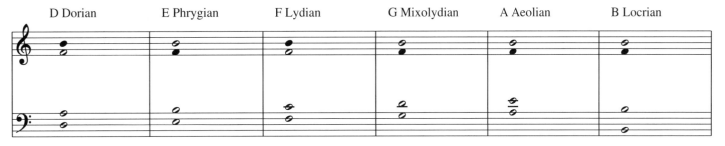

● = characteristic note

The problem with the tritone in modal harmony is not so much the interval itself but the placement of that interval in a voicing in thirds. Voicings in thirds (triads and seventh chords) are so identified with the major and minor modes that their very use promotes tonal rather than modal identity. Bill Evans and Miles Davis must have understood this instinctively at the *Kind of Blue* recording sessions, because Bill Evans makes extensive use of voicings in fourths throughout, especially on "So What."

Voicings in fourths have a more ambiguous quality than voicings in thirds. A quartal "triad" (three-note voicing in perfect fourths) doesn't sound major, minor, augmented, or diminished. In fact, any of the three notes in such a voicing might be the "root" of the chord! This ambiguity has intrigued jazz musicians for more than forty years and is at the heart of the use of these voicings by players and composer/arrangers who hope to sound "modern."

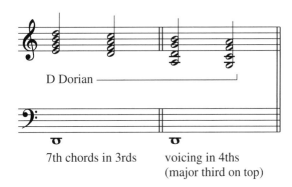

7th chords in 3rds   voicing in 4ths
(major third on top)

It helps to examine the diatonic chords of each mode using three-part voicings in fourths.

D Dorian

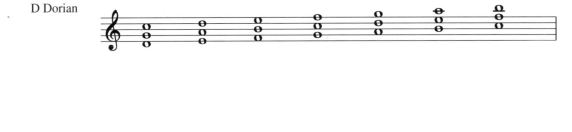

E Phrygian

F Lydian

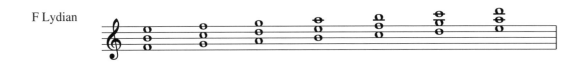

G Mixolydian

A Aeolian

B Locrian

Assigning Roman numerals to these voicings is not particularly helpful because there is no tonic, subdominant, or dominant quality inherent in any of them without a note in the bass. If the modal tonic is added in the bass, most of the voicings will sound "tonic," while one or two voicings may sound vaguely "non-tonic" or like an approach chord. Then, if a note other than the modal tonic is used in the bass, *all* of these voicings will sound non-tonic.

The most important factor in establishing modal orientation is the frequent use of the modal tonic in the bass. This is essential because the tritone is always lurking and threatening to pull you into the relative major mode. As long as the modal tonic is used persistently in the bass voice, all of the diatonic voicings in fourths from the mode can be used above it in virtually any order to provide harmonic fluidity. The use of other notes from the mode in the bass will suggest non-tonic chords that can be used in cadencing to a modal tonic chord.

D Dorian

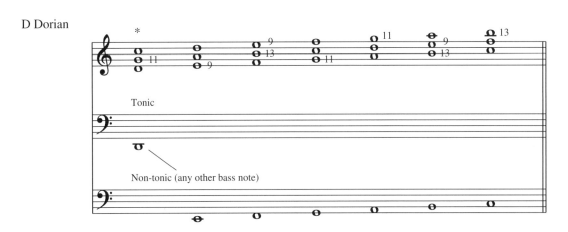

E Phrygian

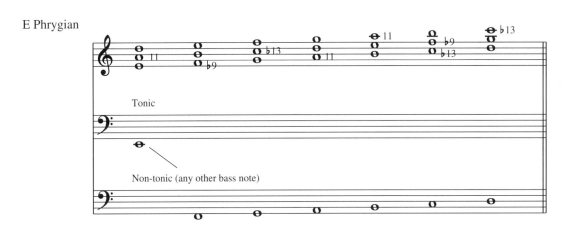

F Lydian

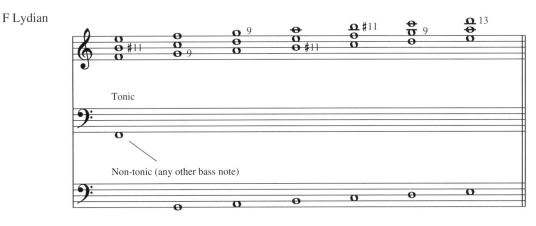

*Another nice thing about using modal voicings in fourths is that each will contain at least one tension of the mode (9, ♭9, 11, ♯11, 13, ♭13).

G Mixolydian

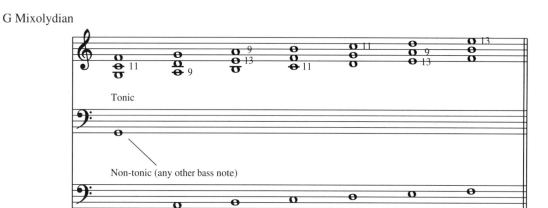

A Aeolian

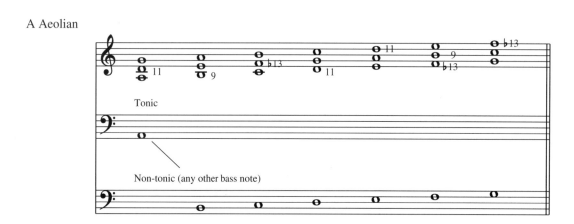

B Locrian

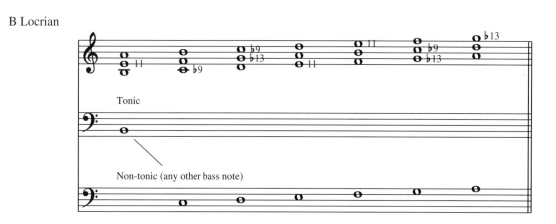

Inverted Voicings in Fourths

Voicings in fourths and their inversions have been used extensively in modal situations by jazz pianists, composers, and arrangers since the early 1960s. A three-part voicing in fourths can be inverted by shifting the bottom note up an octave twice in succession. This results in two new positions of the voicing, which contain the same three notes but in a different intervallic order. Instead of two adjacent fourths, the first inversion contains a fourth on the bottom and a second on top. The second inversion contains a second on the bottom and a fourth on top. (A voicing in thirds has been avoided once again!) The chart on the next page demonstrates inversions of voicings in fourths in D Dorian, E Phrygian, and G Mixolydian.

D Dorian

Voicings in fourths

1st inversion

2nd inversion

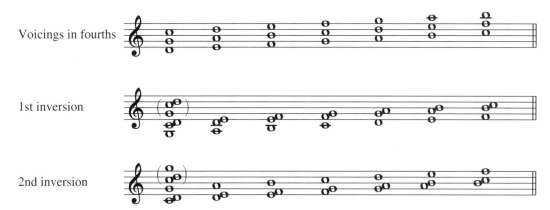

E Phrygian

Voicings in fourths

1st inversion

2nd inversion

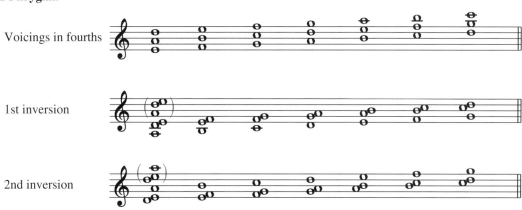

G Mixolydian

Voicings in fourths

1st inversion

2nd inversion

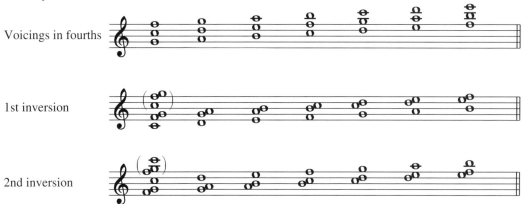

Modal Approach Chords

Chromatic and parallel approach chords are very useful in modal situations, provided they are used only to embellish diatonic chords and not to supplant them. The charts on the next two pages demonstrate how chromatic ("ch") and parallel ("para") approach techniques produce upper and lower neighbor chords that are respectively a half step or a whole step above or below their modal target chords. Double chromatic ("dc") approach is also possible if the parallel approach chord moves first to the chromatic approach chord (as indicated by the horizontal arrows). These approach chords, rather than the secondary dominants of tonal harmony, produce the harmonic universe of the modes in jazz.

As you study the following Harmonic Universe charts, notice that some of the parallel approach chords ("para") are identical to diatonic chords from the mode. These diatonic approach chords help reinforce the mode when used appropriately. On the charts, these "para" chords are checked and labeled in **bold** type.

Harmonic Universe in D Dorian

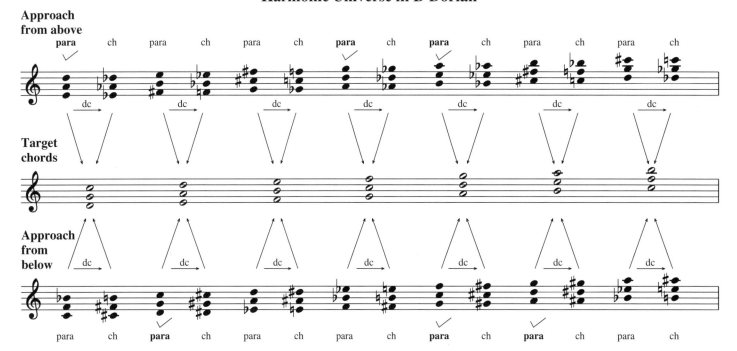

Suggested cadential patterns in the bass are:

Harmonic Universe in E Phrygian

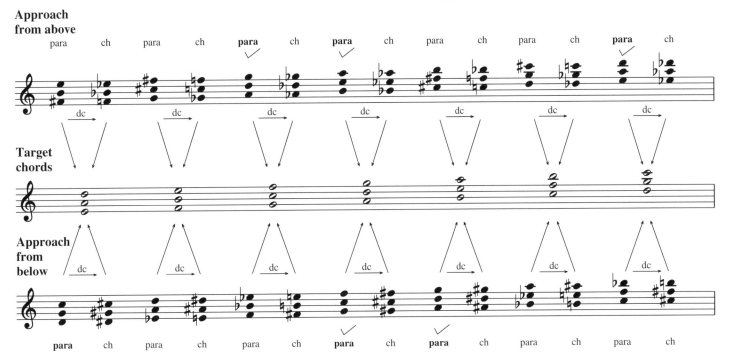

Suggested cadential patterns in the bass are:

Harmonic Universe in G Mixolydian

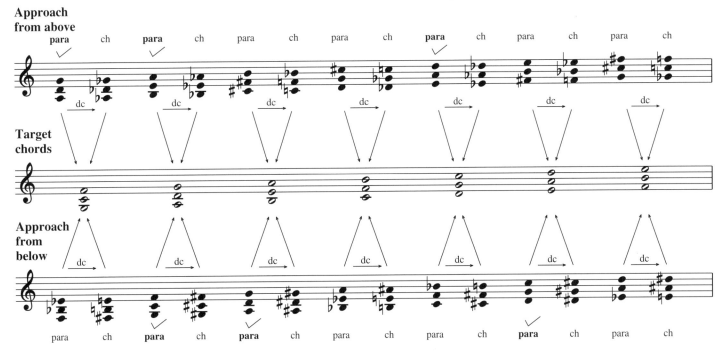

Suggested cadential patterns in the bass are:

Modal Melodies

Modal melodies are usually diatonic. There may be an occasional short chromatic or parallel approach note on a weak beat. Modal melodies should emphasize the tonic of the mode and the characteristic note. Melodic rhythm depends on the tempo and the overall rhythmic groove. Many modal melodies alternate between notes of long duration (of a measure or longer) and short groups of eighth notes.

Observe the next tune, "Any Port in a Storm." Notice that three modes are represented: D Dorian, E Phrygian, and G Mixolydian (sometimes referred to as the "white note" modes because of their relationship to white piano keys). Notice also that the entire piece is written without any chromatics (accidentals outside the respective modes), with the exception of the G-sharps in measures 10 and 11. The G-sharps are borrowed from the Spanish Phrygian scale, in which the major and minor third are used interchangeably.

Notice the repeated references to the respective modal tonics in the bass voice of the piano part. These modal tonics are reinforced above by perfect fifths. Notice that there are also some *non*-tonic notes in the bass voice. The resulting non-tonic approach chords above them are used to surround and reinforce the modal tonic.

The respective modal tonics and characteristic modal notes appear frequently in the melody and are circled for reference.

Any Port in a Storm

Ted Pease

EXERCISES

1. Replicate the charts on pages 65–67 showing voicings in fourths for each scale degree of the designated modes. Indicate non-tonic bass notes. Be sure to play these voicings on the piano.

C Dorian (voicings in fourths)

Tonic

Non-Tonic

G Phrygian (inverted voicings in fourths)

Tonic

Non-Tonic

A♭ Mixolydian (inverted voicings in fourths)

Tonic

Non-Tonic

G Dorian (voicings in fourths)

Tonic

Non-Tonic

F Phrygian (inverted voicings in fourths)

Tonic

Non-Tonic

B♭ Mixolydian (inverted voicings in fourths)

Tonic

Non-Tonic

2. Supply diatonic modal melodies for the following situations. Think scale (mode), not chord change!

G Dorian: medium jazz waltz

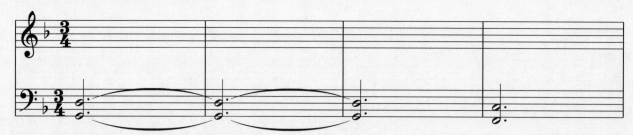

D Phrygian: medium swing

G Lydian: slow ballad

C Mixolydian: fast swing

B Locrian: slow swing

Harmonic Variation via Modal Interchange

Modal interchange occurs when a diatonic chord from one tonality or modality is borrowed for use in another tonality or modality. Modal interchange is used by composers and arrangers when a repetitive chord progression involving II–7, IV, IV–, or V7 needs some reharmonization for the sake of variety.

MODAL INTERCHANGE FROM MINOR TO MAJOR

The following minor-key chords are liberally borrowed via modal interchange for use in the parallel major key (e.g., from C minor to C major).

CHORD	FUNCTION	EXAMPLE IN C MAJOR
II-7($\flat$5)	replaces II–7	D–7($\flat$5)
$\flat$IIIMaj7	replaces IV or V7	E$\flat$Maj7
IV–7 or IV–6	replaces IV	F–7 or F–6
V–7	replaces V7	G–7
$\flat$VIMaj7	replaces IV–	A$\flat$Maj7
$\flat$VII7	replaces IV–	B$\flat$7

MODAL INTERCHANGE FROM MODAL TO MAJOR

The following chord is liberally borrowed from Dorian mode for use in the parallel major key (e.g., from C Dorian to C major):

CHORD	FUNCTION	EXAMPLE IN C MAJOR
V–7	replaces V7	G–7

The following chord is liberally borrowed from Phrygian mode for use in the parallel major key (e.g., from C Phrygian to C major):

CHORD	FUNCTION	EXAMPLE IN C MAJOR
$\flat$IIMaj7	replaces IV–	D$\flat$Maj7

The following chord is liberally borrowed from Lydian mode for use in the parallel major key (e.g., from C Lydian to C major):

CHORD	FUNCTION	EXAMPLE IN C MAJOR
IMaj7($\sharp$11)	tonic alias in C	CMaj7($\sharp$11)

The following chord is liberally borrowed from Mixolydian mode for use in the parallel major key (e.g., from C Mixolydian to C major):

CHORD	FUNCTION	EXAMPLE IN C MAJOR
$\flat$VIIMaj7	replaces IV	B$\flat$Maj7

MODAL INTERCHANGE FROM MAJOR TO MODAL

The following chord is liberally borrowed from Ionian (major) mode for use in the parallel Dorian mode (e.g., from C major to C Dorian):

CHORD	FUNCTION	EXAMPLE IN C DORIAN
IV Maj7	replaces IV7 (avoids tritone)	FMaj7

In the following example, each of the previous examples of modal interchange is written out for aural comparison. In the first measure of each two-measure example, CMaj7 (I) is followed by either II–7, IV, IV–, or V7 for reference. In the second measure of each two-measure example, CMaj7 is followed by a related modal interchange chord from the preceding list. (In the final example, the I chord is I–7 in Dorian mode.)

It is suggested that you play these examples at the piano several times in order to train your ear to hear them.

Modal Interchange

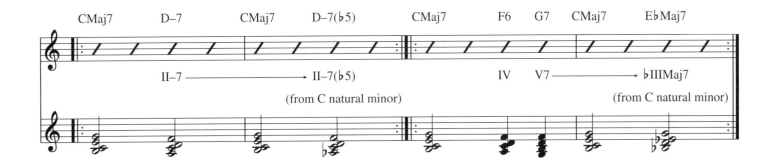

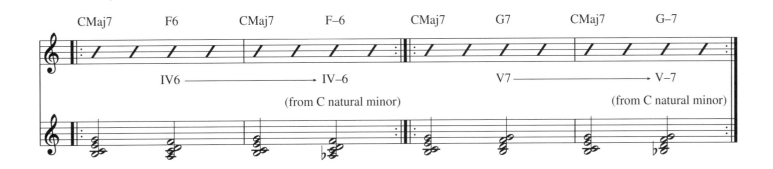

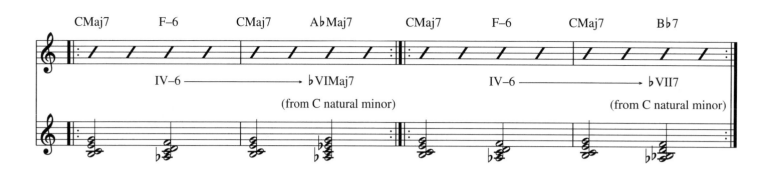

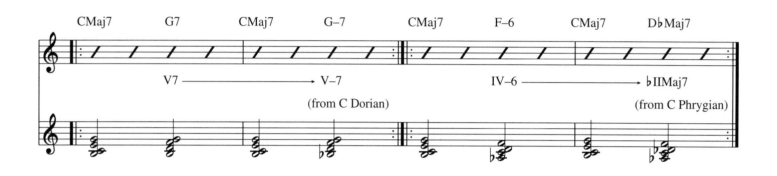

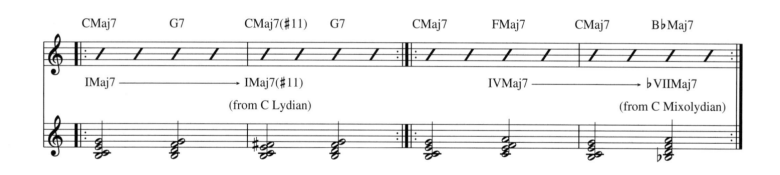

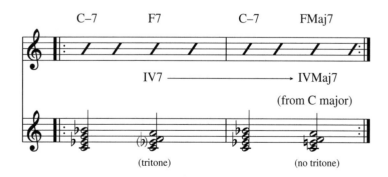

EXERCISE

Use modal interchange chords at the spots marked with a box. Compare your choices to the original.

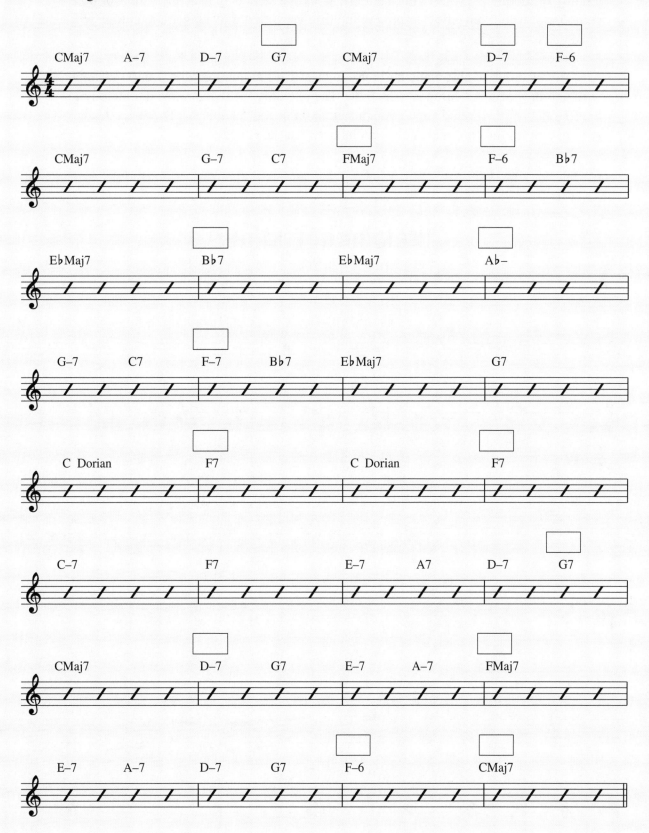

Chromatic Harmony

Chromatic harmony is produced when two chords are connected by one or more half-steps. This may happen in tonal contexts (as in the resolution of the tritone), but it is more dramatic when the result is a new chord from a distantly related or unrelated tonality or modality. Hence, chromatic harmony has held a special attraction for jazz composers, who often enjoy surprising the listener with abrupt transitions into new tonal or modal territory.

An early example of chromatic harmony in classical literature can be found in Chopin's "Prelude in E Minor," composed in 1836. The example below contains the melody to the first half of the Prelude and an approximation of the "changes." The voice-leading sketch outlines the chromatic connections between the chords.

(See also "And There You Are," page 189.)

Prelude in E Minor

Chopin

Harmonic Rhythm (and Density)

Chord progressions in jazz are designed to move at a pace that coincides with the overall meter of a piece. In 4/4 time, harmonic rhythms tend to occur in multiples of two beats. Thus, there are harmonic rhythms of two beats in the *a* section of "Scooter." (See page 128.)

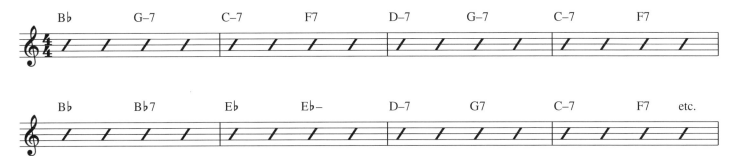

There are harmonic rhythms of four beats (and then two beats) in "After Breakfast." (See page 119.)

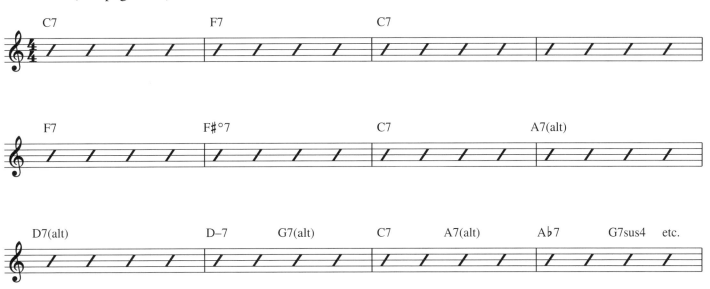

There are harmonic rhythms of eight beats (i.e., two measures) in the bridge of "Scooter":

Longer harmonic durations are found in such modal tunes as "So What" by Miles Davis and "Impressions" by John Coltrane. Both of these tunes have sustained "harmonies" of eight and sixteen measures, but those "harmonies" are really just verticalized Dorian scales. Even longer harmonic durations can be found in early fusion pieces that are based on sustained rhythmic grooves (as in selections from *Bitches Brew* by Miles Davis). In effect, these pieces have no harmonic rhythm. They achieve effectiveness through rhythmic rather than harmonic motion. (See "With All Due Respect," page 193.)

Harmonic rhythms in 3/4 tend to occur in multiples of three beats (See "For Bill," page 141.):

Harmonic rhythms in 5/4 are usually subdivided into 3+2 or 2+3 (See "Full House," page 180.):

Harmonic rhythms in 7/4 are usually subdivided into 4+3 or 3+4 (See "Uno, Dos, Tres...," page 181.):

Harmonic cross rhythms are sometimes used. In measures 33–39 of "Samba de Goofed" (page 155), two measures of 4/4 time are twice subdivided 3+5 and then subdivided 3+3+2:

Modulations

One of the easiest ways to create variety and interest in a composition is to use a modulation. Modulations may be abrupt and unconfirmed (as in the rapid series of keys-of-the-moment in "Giant Steps" by John Coltrane), temporary, but confirmed (as in going from D♭ major to D major in the bridge of "Body and Soul" by Johnny Green), or permanent (as in a key change moving into a new episode of an extended composition such as "Harlem" by Duke Ellington). In any case, a modulation represents a fresh start and a chance for the composer to present familiar or new musical material in a different light.

Modulations to flat keys sound progressively darker as you move down in a cycle of fifths: F–B♭–E♭–A♭–D♭–G♭–C♭. Modulations to sharp keys sound progressively brighter as you move up in a cycle of fifths: G–D–A–E–B–F♯–C♯ . The key of C sounds brighter when coming from a flat key and darker when coming from a sharp key. (In general, jazz composers favor flat keys, plus the keys of C and G, because they are more comfortable and familiar for saxophones and brass instruments.) Modulations can move along this continuum in either direction so that the desired response is obtained. This response is subjective, of course, but it can be reinforced by moving the melody up to enhance brightness or down to enhance darkness during the modulation. You can also neutralize the modulation somewhat by moving the melody in opposition to the modulation.

Another way to create modulatory interest is to move from minor to major (increasing brightness, as in going from C minor to A♭ major when entering the bridge of "Angel Eyes" by Matt Dennis), or from major to minor (increasing darkness, as in going from G major back to C minor coming out of the bridge of that same tune).

Modulations up a half-step (e.g., C to D♭) enhance brightness and intensity. Modulations down a half-step (e.g., A♭ to G) release tension.

Modal modulations also create interest. Modes can be described in subjective terms as having a dark to bright spectrum moving in a cycle of fifths from Locrian (the darkest) through Phrygian, Aeolian, Dorian, Mixolydian, and Ionian, to Lydian (the brightest).

Contemporary jazz composers delight in moving rapidly through different tonal areas without stopping to smell the flowers. In Coltrane's "Giant Steps," there are ten "modulations" in the space of sixteen measures! In other cases, the tonic chord of a tonal area is deliberately avoided to keep the listener (and sometimes the players!) off balance. A tune such as "Nefertiti" by Wayne Shorter is so harmonically ambiguous that there is no key signature on the lead sheet in *The New Real Book* (published in 1988 by Sher Music Co., page 232).

Cadential Modulations (New I Chord Realized)

1. **Permanent**: confirmed with a change of key signature.

   a. Direct: uses a pivot chord, which has a defined function in both keys. In the following example, the A♭7 is the pivot chord, serving as the ♭VI7 in C and V7 in D♭.

Cadences to C and D♭ are explicit.

   b. Indirect: no pivot chord.

Cadence to D♭ is explicit, but there is no prior cadence to C. E♭–7 is not a pivot chord because it has no apparent function in C major. A♭7 is not a pivot chord because the key of D♭ has already been suggested by E♭–7.)

2. **Transient**: short-lived unconfirmed key-of-the-moment situations; key signature not changed; sometimes referred to as "tonic systems."

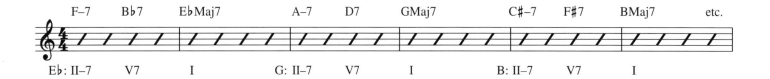

Non-cadential Modulations (New I Chord Not Realized or Confirmed)

1. **Transient**: I chord is absent; short-lived unconfirmed key-of-the-moment situations.

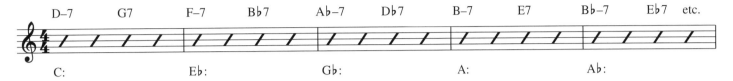

2. **Constant structures**: parallel harmonic construction; may or may not suggest key(s)-of-the-moment

3. **Random or ambiguous** (enhanced by chromatic harmony)

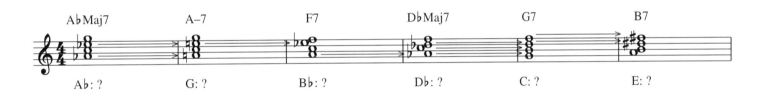

EXERCISES

Create cadential modulation scenarios for the following, using chord symbols.

1. **Permanent** (confirmed with a change of key signature)

   a. Direct (uses a pivot chord):

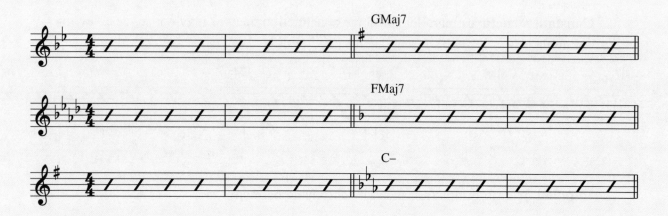

   b. Indirect (no pivot chord):

2. **Transient** (unconfirmed key-of-the-moment situations):

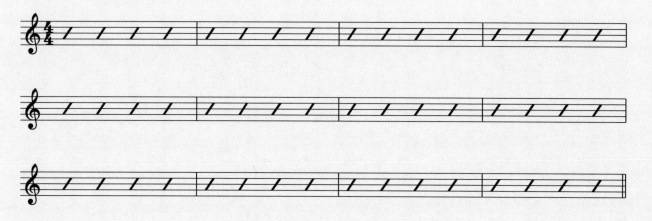

Create non-cadential modulation scenarios for the following using chord symbols.

1. **Transient** (I chord is absent; short-lived key-of-the-moment situations):

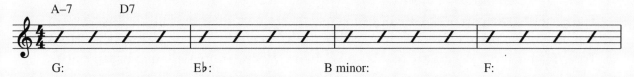

2. **Constant structures** (parallel harmonic construction):

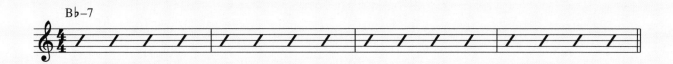

3. **Random or ambiguous** (using chromatic harmony—one chord per measure. Indicate the chromatic connectors):

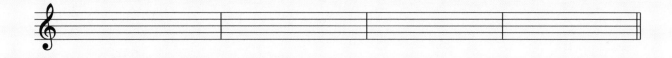

OSTINATO

An ostinato is a motif (riff) that is repeated persistently in the bass voice. Ostinatos are very common in Latin tunes and tunes that are in unusual meters.

The earliest examples of the use of ostinatos in jazz come from the left-hand patterns of boogie-woogie piano players such as Meade "Lux" Lewis in the late 1920s. (His "Honky Tonk Train Blues" is a classic in this style.) In the 1940s, Dizzy Gillespie began using Afro-Cuban rhythms in some of his compositions and arrangements. Two of his most well-known compositions from that period, "A Night in Tunisia" and "Manteca," contain ostinatos in the *a* section of their respective forms.

In the 1950s and 1960s, Dave Brubeck and Don Ellis used ostinatos in unusual meters such as 5/4, 7/4, 9/8, and 11/8 to help anchor the rhythmic groove of their compositions. Wayne Shorter's composition "Footprints" contains an ostinato in 6/4. In the 1970s and 1980s, ostinatos were prevalent in jazz-rock and fusion. Herbie Hancock's composition "Chameleon" and Joe Zawinul's "Birdland" contain well-known ostinatos that help make these pieces instantly recognizable.

No Way

Ted Pease

Notice that the ostinato can be repositioned to fit a new chord.

EXERCISE

Add an appropriate ostinato to the following melody.

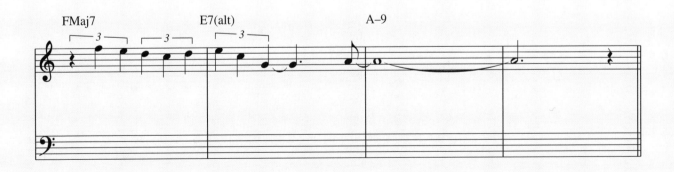

Inversions and Other "Slash" Chords

The role of bass lines in jazz composition and arranging became increasingly important in the 1970s and 1980s. The electric bass assumed a dominant role in the rhythm section of fusion groups such as Weather Report and Return to Forever. Inversions and "slash" chords became increasingly common as composers and arrangers searched for prominent ways to feature the bass. Inversions are indicated by the principal chord symbol followed by a diagonal slash and a designated bass note—e.g., D7/F♯ for a D7 chord in first inversion. Other so-called "slash" chords such as D/F are used to produce a more ambiguous and dissonant sound. Inversions and slash chords highlight the bass line by emphasizing notes other than the root and help to create a sense of counterpoint between the melody and the bass line.

Slash chords such as FMaj7/E or A♭Maj7/D are interesting because they provide chord changes that are slightly out of focus. The resulting dissonance sounds more dramatic than the standard root-position orientation. It is interesting to note that the more dissonant the relationship between the chord and the bass note, the more a composer/arranger is liable to use it. Combinations that produce dissonant intervals, such as the major seventh and the minor ninth, between the bass and one of the chord tones above are now quite prevalent both in tunes and in extended compositions.

Inversions and slash chords prove especially useful when simple chord progressions are reharmonized. This simple example can be transformed via the use of inversions and other slash chords:

Borrowed Time

Ted Pease

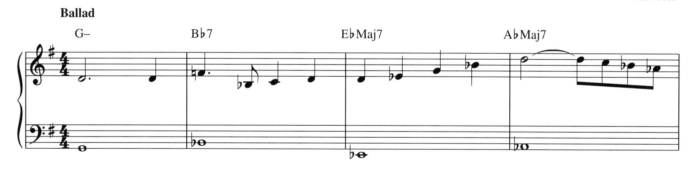

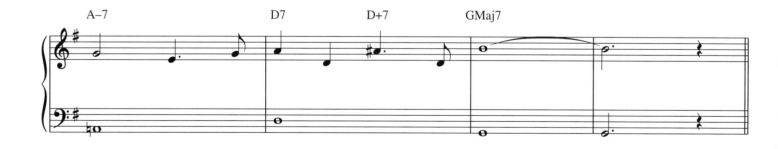

Here is the transformation:

Borrowed Time (Reharmonized)

Ted Pease

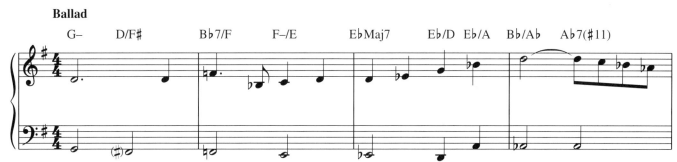

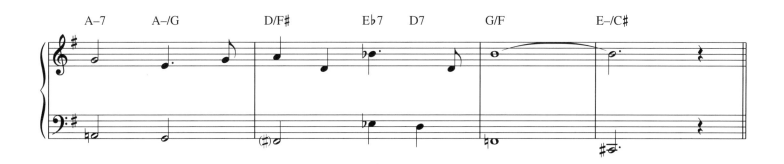

Pedal Point and Constant Structures

A pedal point is another effective harmonic device. A single note (the pedal point), which is often the tonic or the dominant of the scale or mode, is sustained or repeated, usually in the bass voice. Melody and/or harmony move against the pedal point in the upper register, creating consonant and dissonant relationships with it. Constant structures (parallel voice leading of triads, voicings in fourths, or any other voicing) are frequently used over a pedal point for intros, interludes, and endings.

12   (Major triads over D♭ pedal)   (Major 7ths over D♭ pedal)

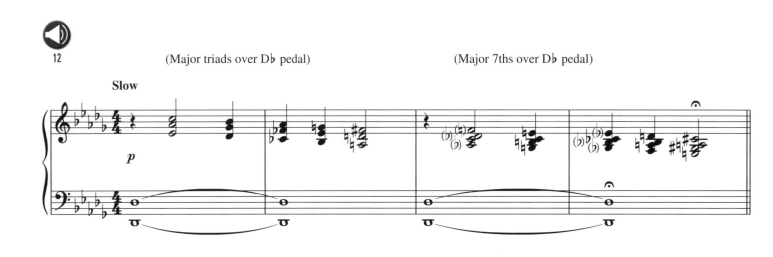

13   (Voicings in fourths over G pedal)

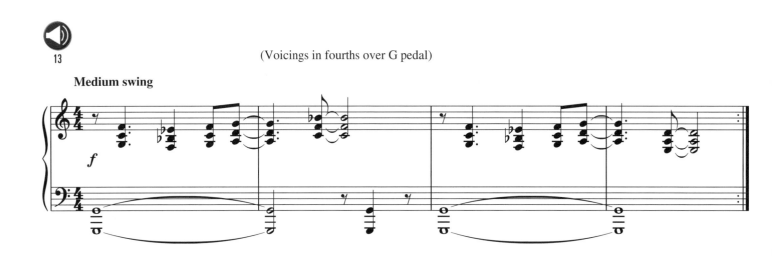

EXERCISE

Write two intros using designated constant structures over the given pedal point and under the given lead line.

Complete the following examples of various constant structures (to be played over a C pedal). Play and compare them at the piano.

Example

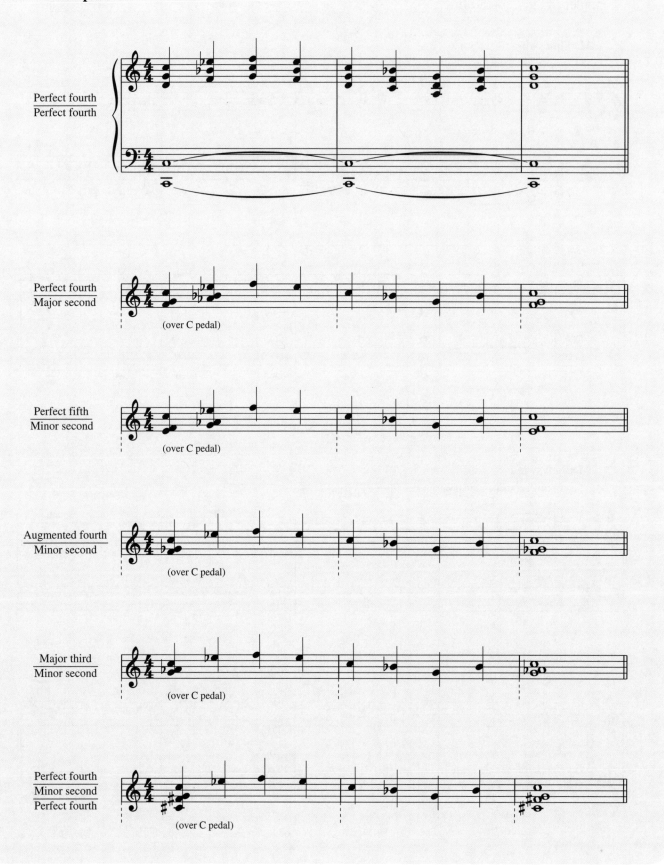

Pedal Point and Pandiatonicism

Pandiatonicism is produced by strictly confining harmonic material to a given scale (i.e., with no chromatic, or out-of-scale, intrusion). This concept can be applied to any scale, but it is most commonly used in tonal and modal contexts. The technique is similar to constant structures, but the intervals of all voicings are adjusted so as to conform to the scale of the moment. The spacing may be uniform or variable.

Example 1: Tonal context with uniform spacing

Medium swing

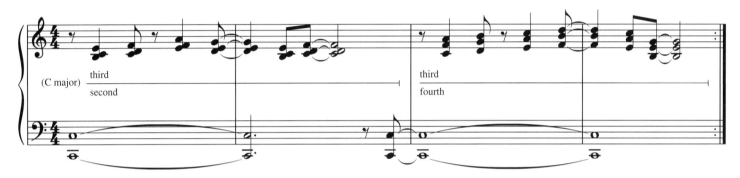

Example 2: Modal context with variable spacings

Medium swing

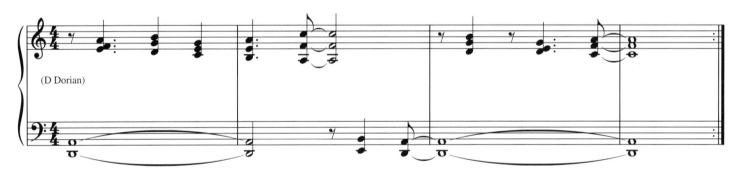

EXERCISES

Complete the following pandiatonic examples. Play and compare them at the piano.

Slow

fifth/second

(F major)

Medium swing

fourth/second

(G major)

Medium fast

fourth/fourth

(C Dorian)

Fast

fourth/second

(A Phrygian)

Harmonization

Okay, so you've written a melodic masterpiece. What about the chords to go with it? Choosing chords to go with a melody may seem daunting at first because there are so many possibilities. But that is part of the enjoyment of composing: CHOICE!

If you are a pianist or guitarist, it is likely that you have been composing melody and harmony simultaneously on your instrument. Even so, there are probably moments when you are unsure as to the desired chord quality, or what degree of tension to use, so you have paused to consider various possibilities in a methodical way. If you are a wind player, the choice of a chord is even more problematic if you are not as used to thinking of chords on your instrument and have limited keyboard skills.

At first it seems that there are only two ways to approach the task of harmonizing a melody. One is to rely on the familiar tonal and modal relationships in conventional jazz harmony discussed earlier in this section. The I chord is the boss, and all the other chords in the tonal or modal universe are used in service to it. There is diatonic harmony; there are secondary dominants and their substitutes along with related II–7 chords, etc. The other way is to free yourself of those limitations and proceed with the concept that any chord can follow any other chord. This is fun, but it can result in either tortured chord progressions or harmonic incoherence. The best way is to combine these two approaches—use conventional chord progressions to provide clarity, but utilize unexpected harmonic twists and turns to promote variety and interest.

Obviously the choice of a chord will depend upon its compatibility with the melody. Notes of long duration (longer than a quarter note) should be chord tones or tensions of the chosen chord. Shorter notes may just be embellishments—approach notes if they move by step to a target note, or escape tones if they don't.

Ask yourself: What key or mode is my melody in? Will diatonic harmony work? Does my melody arpeggiate a chord or part of a chord? Is a major, minor, or modal scale suggested by my melody? If not, consider the possibilities that emerge if you assign the first important whole note or half note of the tune to a major, minor, or dominant chord by making that note 1, 3, 5, 7, 9, 11, or 13 of the potential chord. What kind of a chord should it be? Major 7? Minor 7? Dominant 7? Does the style of your tune play a role in that decision? This is where your ear, and perhaps your instrument, comes into play. Making choices without confirming them audibly is risky!

Consider the many possibilities that exist to harmonize the note C. The chart on the next page lists a number of them.

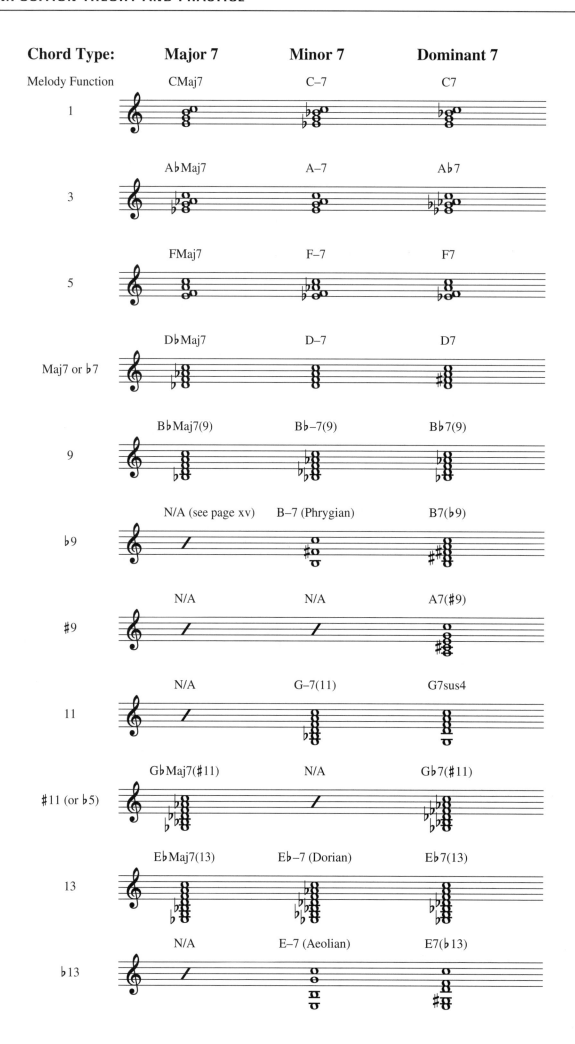

Sometimes a melody will arpeggiate a chord. The arpeggio may have the chord in root position, as in the following example (E–7). Notice that other solutions may exist for the same arpeggio. If you think of the first note (E) as the third of CMaj7, or as the fifth of A–7, or as the major seventh of FMaj7, or as T13 of G7, you get four additional harmonization possibilities.

= E–7, CMaj9, A–11, FMaj7(♯11), G13

Here are two other melodic fragments consisting of broken chords and some possible solutions for harmonizing them.

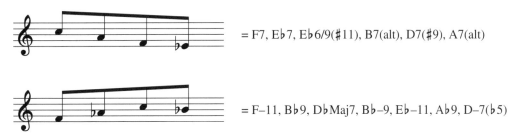

= F7, E♭7, E♭6/9(♯11), B7(alt), D7(♯9), A7(alt)

= F–11, B♭9, D♭Maj7, B♭–9, E♭–11, A♭9, D–7(♭5)

On a scalewise passage such as the following, see if you can determine the key-of-the-moment. Then choose harmonies from that harmonic universe.

= C6, D–9, FMaj7, G9sus4, A–7

When you have decided which chord to start with, move on to the next important melody note (a whole note, a half note, an accented note, a note preceded by or followed by a leap). Will it receive a new chord? What is the harmonic rhythm of your tune going to be: sixteen beats (four measures), eight beats (two measures), four beats (one measure), or two beats (half a measure)? Does the tempo of the tune play a role? Look for guide tones that can connect the two chords together, especially if your melody leaps between them.

Below is a melodic fragment that has been given the treatment outlined on the previous page. As you can see, there are seven solutions offered. (There are undoubtedly many more.)

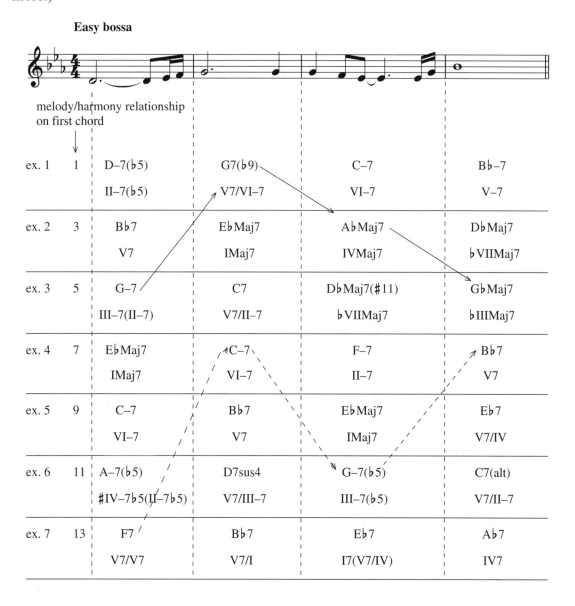

Additional solutions can be discovered by interchanging chords amongst and between the respective columns. The solid-line arrow shows one such possibility. (Some choices may prove to be less effective. The dotted-line arrow produces a progression that is a little too scattered and dysfunctional. Use your ears when you experiment!)

EXERCISES

Harmonize (add chord changes to) the following four-measure melodic fragments.
(These examples need not cadence to a I chord.)

Ballad

Easy Latin

Samba

Medium swing

Slow jazz waltz

Fast swing

Add appropriate chord changes to the following melodies.

Supply chord changes for the following tune.

Harmonique

Ted Pease

Reharmonization

The initial harmonization of a melody is not always the final one that a composer or arranger settles on. In fact, a melody may go through several harmonic incarnations before the final chord changes are chosen. We have already seen how a single melody can accommodate many different harmonic solutions. Even after a lead sheet has been in circulation for some time you can always find piano players who will reharmonize the melody. Indeed, there may be subsequent situations where even the composer finds that the initial harmonization needs to be rethought.

Reharmonization is also used as a development technique in composition and arranging. Once the exposition of a composition or arrangement has taken place, later statements of important themes can be revitalized through reharmonization. Reharmonization is simply one more tool that composers and arrangers have at their disposal.

There are various ways of approaching a reharmonization situation, from simple to more complex and sophisticated. We will use the following example as a starting point.

1. Upgrade from triads to seventh chords and/or ninth chords.

2. Embellish the existing progression with other functional chords from the corresponding harmonic universe (related II—7s, secondary dominants, substitute dominants, etc.).

3. Look for contiguous (back-to-back) II – Vs that are compatible with the melody.

4. Use modal interchange chords (see page 76).

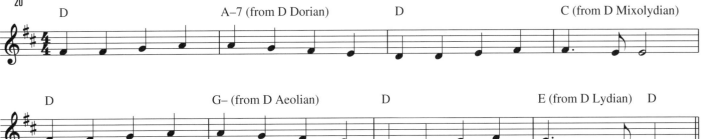

5. Choose chords that increase the level of melodic and harmonic tension.

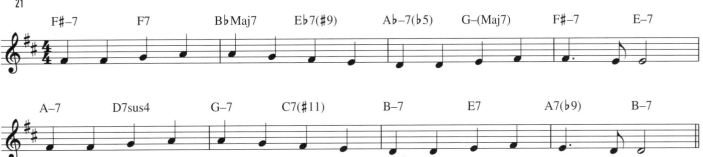

6. Create a stepwise bass line (up or down) and write chords above it that are compatible with the melody. (Functional harmony need not apply, so any chord can follow any other chord—melody permitting. *However*, use your ears!)

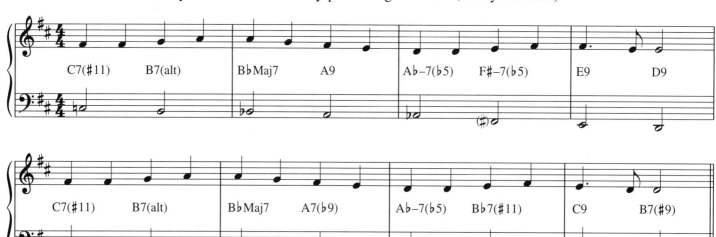

7. Use constant structures over a pedal point.

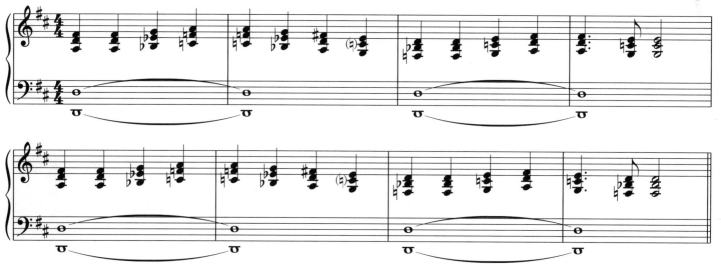

8. Use pandiatonic structures over a pedal point.

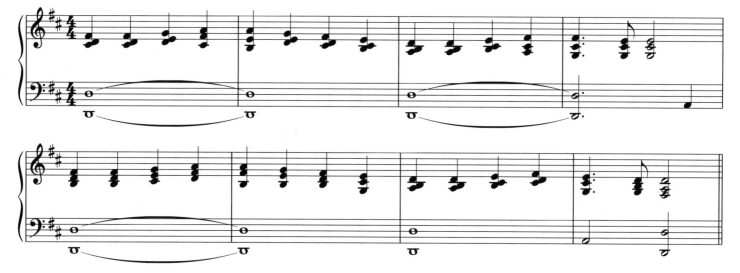

6. Create a stepwise bass line (up or down) and write chords that are compatible with the melody.

7. Use constant structures over a pedal point.

8. Use pandiatonic structures over a pedal point.

EXERCISE

Reharmonize the chord changes to the following well-known melody using the suggested procedures from the previous pages.

1. Upgrade from triads to seventh chords and/or ninth chords.

2. Embellish with other functional chords from the corresponding harmonic universe.

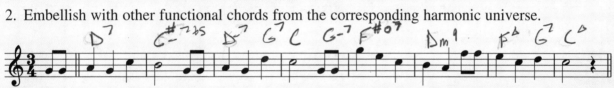

3. Look for contiguous (back-to-back) II – Vs that are compatible with the melody.

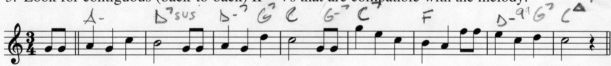

4. Use modal interchange chords.

5. Choose chords that increase the level of melodic and harmonic tension.

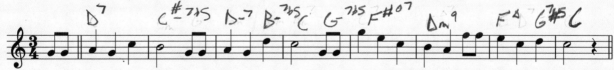

6. Create a stepwise bass line (up or down) and write chords that are compatible with the melody.

7. Use constant structures over a pedal point.

8. Use pandiatonic structures over a pedal point.

Source Material—Harmonic Considerations

TONAL HARMONY—MAJOR KEY ORIENTATION
See "Catch Me If You Can," page 54.
A Child is Born (Thad Jones)—B♭ major
Boplicity (Miles Davis)—F major
It's Only Music (Gary Willis)—A♭ major
Perdido (Juan Tizol)—B♭ major
Satin Doll (Duke Ellington)—C major
Seven Steps to Heaven (Victor Feldman)—F major
Yesterday and Today (Dario Eskanazi)—F major

TONAL HARMONY—MINOR KEY ORIENTATION
See "Minor Differences," page 59.
Autumn Leaves (Joseph Kosma)—G minor
Django (John Lewis)—F minor
Keep It Moving (Wynton Kelly)—F minor
Loco Motiv (Larry Gales)—D minor
Song for My Father (Horace Silver)—F minor
Whisper Not (Benny Golson)—C minor

MODAL HARMONY AND MODAL MELODIES
See "Any Port in a Storm," page 71.
All Blues (Miles Davis)—G Mixolydian, G Dorian
Don't Let It Go (Vincent Herring)—E♭ Lydian, G Mixolydian, F Mixolydian
Impressions (John Coltrane)—D Dorian, E♭ Dorian
Nardis (Miles Davis)—E Phrygian, C Ionian
Pursuance (John Coltrane)—B♭ Aeolian
So What (Miles Davis)—D Dorian, E♭ Dorian

HARMONIC VARIATION VIA MODAL INTERCHANGE
Jeannine (Duke Pearson)—A♭ Dorian to A♭ major
No More Blues (Antonio Carlos Jobim)—D minor to D major
Stolen Moments (Oliver Nelson)—C Dorian to C major

CHROMATIC HARMONY
See "And There You Are," page 189.
At Night (Marc Copland)
Beauty Secrets (Kenny Werner)
Epiphany (Denny Zeitlin)
Dreams (Billy Childs)
I'll Remember August (Ralph Towner)
Stepping Stone (Steve Masakowski)

HARMONIC RHYTHM (AND DENSITY)
1. Active (See "Move It," page 121.)
    Blues for Alice (Charles Parker)
    Giant Steps (John Coltrane)
    Daahoud (Clifford Brown)

2. Inactive (See "Rascals," page 134.)
   Impressions (John Coltrane)
   Little Sunflower (Freddie Hubbard)
   Maiden Voyage (Herbie Hancock)
   So What (Miles Davis)

MODULATIONS

See references in the text.

OSTINATO

See "No Way," page 88.
Afro-Centric (Joe Henderson)
Aisha (McCoy Tyner)
Birdland (Joe Zawinul)
Black Narcissus (Joe Henderson)
Fly with the Wind (McCoy Tyner)
Loco Motiv (Larry Gales)
Memory and Desire (Billy Childs)
Nutville (Horace Silver)

INVERSIONS AND OTHER "SLASH" CHORDS

See "And There You Are," page 189.
The Beauty of All Things (Laurence Hobgood)
Cafe (Egberto Gismonti)
Cassidae (John Scofield)
Delgado (Eddie Gomez)
Like Father, Like Son (Billy Childs)
Little Wind (Geri Allen)
Memory and Desire (Billy Childs)
Paladia (Steve Masakowski)

PEDAL POINT

The Beauty of All Things (Laurence Hobgood)
Capuccino (Chick Corea)
Cirrus (Bobby Hutcherson)
Epiphany (Denny Zeitlin)
Firm Roots (Cedar Walton)
I'll Remember August (Ralph Towner)
Naima (John Coltrane)
Paladia (Steve Masakowski)
Truth (Bob Mintzer)

CHAPTER 3
Blues and Song Form

Form

In order to be intelligible, music needs structure. In the absence of structure, collections of pitches and rhythms can seem random and chaotic. Ever since human beings began to perceive the sounds around them (or those that they could make themselves) as "music"—wind, thunder, rain, the heartbeat, breathing, vocalizing, footsteps, chopping, clapping—there has been the impulse to somehow organize these sounds into patterns for communication purposes. Pitch and rhythm make up the atoms and molecules of music, but without form they remain amorphous and indistinct.

We can make an educated guess that the first "music" was probably rhythm. Without the rhythms of the heartbeat and breathing, we wouldn't exist. There are other rhythms all around us—day and night, the changing seasons, phases of the moon—that organize the passage of time into perceptible phenomena that help us define our existence. We can create rhythms by clapping our hands together. We can make those sounds louder and more insistent by beating a drum. And we can make rhythms slower or faster to express certain feelings.

We can also make sounds with our voice. If talking is not sufficient for conveying a certain emotion, we can yell or cry out. If we control the pitch and volume of these vocal sounds, perhaps the nature of the emotion becomes clearer, and we have successfully communicated something. If we go a step further and add proper intonation and nuance, melody can be created. We can sing melodies and we can play them on musical instruments. If we are joined by others in these endeavors, polyphony may happen. If we agree to make different sounds together in the same rhythm, harmony may happen. And so on.

There is still an important element missing in all of this: how to organize these sounds into a timeframe that has a beginning, a middle, and an end, because if we do that, we have music composition! And it is this organizational challenge that brings us to a discussion of form.

Some general observations can be made about form in jazz. The most common jazz form is ABA, where A is the melody, or "head," B is the improvised solo or solos, and A is the melody again. (This is roughly analogous to sonata form in classical music where A is the exposition, B is the development, and A is the recapitulation.) The A section (the "head") of a jazz piece usually exhibits one of a number of shorter song forms such as *ab, aaba, abac, abca, abcd,* or the blues. If the improvised solo section utilizes the same form as that of the "head," the piece as a whole can be described as "theme and variations."

A diagram of a typical jazz presentation is:

Exposition	**Development**	**Recapitulation**
"head"	solos	"head"
A (*aaba*)	B (*aaba*)	A (*aaba*)
theme	variations	theme

In the above scenario, the jazz composer creates the theme (the "head," also referred to as "the tune"), and the soloists then improvise on the harmonic form ("the changes") that underlies the theme. In effect, the soloists recompose the theme spontaneously each time they pass through the harmonic form. After the solos, the performers play the head again to conclude the presentation.

Until the 1960s, the most common length for jazz tunes other than blues was 32 measures. This was probably because jazz musicians got used to playing (and sometimes recomposing) popular songs from Broadway shows by George Gershwin, Cole Porter, Jerome Kern, and others in the 1920s and 1930s. These composers favored 32-measure *aaba* and *abac* song forms (although Cole Porter in particular sometimes used much longer forms on tunes such as "Begin the Beguine"). Consequently, many so-called jazz "standards" written in the 1930s, 1940s, and 1950s are 32 measures long and are based on *aaba* or *abac* song form.

Since 1960 or so, jazz composers have made use of many other song forms and lengths. In particular, through-composed tunes have become more common. Through-composed tunes (their forms often designated as *abcd*) rely on motivic manipulation rather than phrase repetition for unity and coherence. A good example of a through-composed jazz tune is "Dolphin Dance" by Herbie Hancock.

Episodic pieces have also become more common. Episodic pieces contain separate and distinct sections that may contain their own specific motifs, themes, and moods. "Birdland" by Joe Zawinul is a good example of an episodic jazz composition.

Jazz composers sometimes use extended forms for larger, more ambitious pieces. The following is a diagram of a hypothetical extended piece:

Introduction ‖ Theme ‖ Development of the theme ‖ Interlude ‖
Solo section ‖ Interlude ‖ Solo section ‖ Interlude and modulation ‖
Further development of the theme ‖ Solo section ‖
Further development and primary climax ‖
Shortened theme recapitulation ‖ Coda

This chapter deals with the blues and various song forms. Chapter 7 deals with episodic form, and Chapter 9 deals with extended form. The first order of business will be to write some jazz tunes. In the pages that follow, you will be given background information on the blues, *aaba* form, *abac* form, *abca* form, and *abcd* form. There are examples that you can listen to on the audio, and you will get a chance to compose tunes using these representative forms. Later, we will move on to larger and more complex forms.

The Blues

The blues is the best place for aspiring jazz composers to get some initial writing experience. The blues is a short form (12 measures), it is based on a reasonably simple chord progression, and melodic traditions are well defined.

First, some historical perspective. In its early stages, the blues was primarily a vocal idiom. Through the blues, an individual singer could relate what was on his mind while accompanying himself on the guitar or perhaps the harmonica. Virtually every expression of human emotion can be found in traditional vocal blues, from happy excitement to abject despair, but the emphasis has always been on life's hard times. Subject matter often includes ironic references to lust, sex, money, material possessions, travel, loneliness, ill health, envy, or greed.

The roots of the blues go all the way back to 19th-century shouts, field hollers, and work songs. The history of the blues then parallels the history of jazz. The blues and jazz have always been separate and distinct idioms, but there has been a great deal of crossover between them over the years. Suffice it to say that the blues in all its myriad forms has permeated every aspect of American popular music and is still spreading throughout the world.

Without blues influences, popular music in general would sound quite different. The blues has given us the blues scale with its "blue notes"—the lowered 3rd and the lowered 7th (and sometimes the lowered 5th).

In addition to their use in jazz, blue notes are used in virtually every other form of popular music, from rock to country-and-western to love songs and ballads.

BLUES: HARMONIC FORM

In general, traditional blues form occurs as follows:

1st phrase: Tonic (four measures)
2nd phrase: Subdominant (two measures); Tonic (two measures)
3rd phrase: Dominant (two measures); Tonic (two measures)

To this basic harmonic form, jazz musicians have added a myriad of embellishment chords, reharmonizations, and substitute chords, some of which are shown in the following examples.

Major Blues Form

NOTE: Any or all of the chords in parentheses may be used.

Bebop Variation

Minor Blues Form

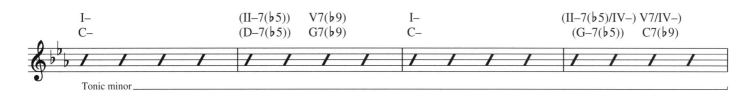

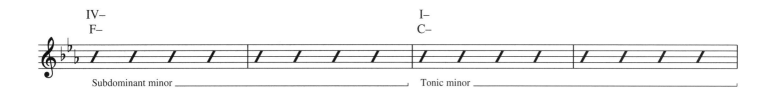

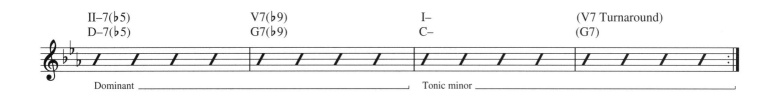

Variation

Modal Blues Form

I

Tonic _____

not I   I

Non-tonic _____   Tonic _____

not I   I

Non-tonic _____   Tonic _____

Sample Dorian Blues

D–7

G7sus4   D–7

A7sus4   G7sus4   D–7

Sample Phrygian Blues

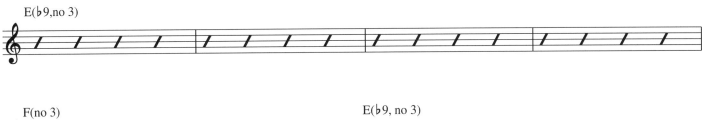

Sample Mixolydian Blues

Variation

16-Bar Blues

In effect, measures 9–10 of the standard 12-bar form are played three times. (Chords in parenthesis are optional.) An example is "Watermelon Man" by Herbie Hancock.

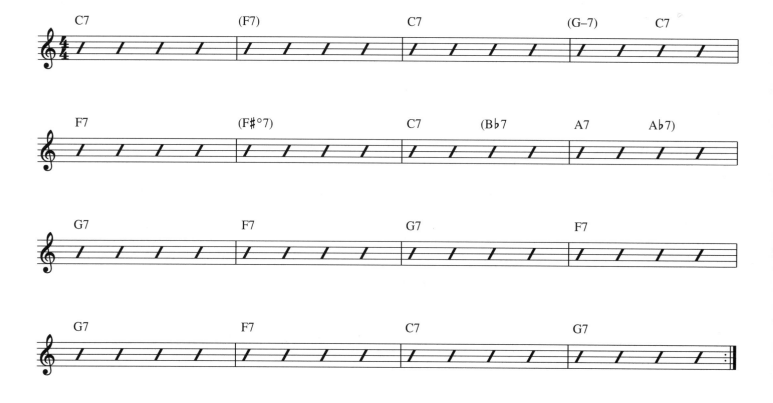

24-Bar Blues

The 24-bar blues form can be created by doubling the harmonic rhythm of the standard 12-bar form. This can be done in 4/4 (as in "Nutville" by Horace Silver) or 3/4 (as in "Blues for Yna Yna" by Gerald Wilson), and in major, minor, or modal contexts.

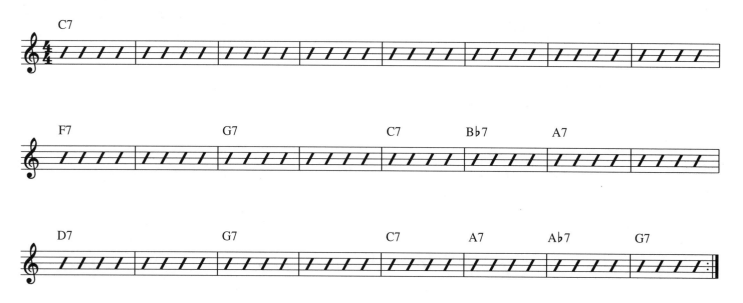

BLUES: MELODIC FORM

Blues melodies follow one of three different forms: *aaa*, *aab*, and *abc*, with each letter representing a four-measure phrase. In the *aaa* (or riff) type blues, the same four-measure melodic figure is sounded three times over the underlying chord progression. "C-jam Blues" (Duke Ellington) and "Sonny Moon for Two" (Sonny Rollins) each consist of a four-measure riff which is played three times.

aaa (**riff-type**): Major key, using C minor pentatonic scale

After Breakfast

Ted Pease

The *aab* blues form is derived from old-style vocal blues. In that style, each four-measure phrase is subdivided, with the vocalist taking the first two measures and a responding instrumentalist taking the second two measures in a sympathetic conversational manner. In a modern context, a typical verse might resemble the following:

> My rent's not paid, got no place to go; (instrumental commentary)
> I said, the rent's not paid, got no place to go; (instrumental commentary)
> (It's) been a long time, since I felt so low. (instrumental commentary)

The instrumental *aab* type blues offers an initial riff twice and then concludes with a different riff that approximates the musical "punch line" in vocal blues. Well-known early vocal examples of *aab* blues form include "St. Louis Blues" (W.C. Handy), which was one of the earliest published blues, and "Roll 'em Pete" (Pete Johnson). More recent well-known instrumental examples include "Now's the Time" (Charlie Parker) and "The Intimacy of the Blues" (Billy Strayhorn).

aab: Minor key, using the D minor blues scale

Any Friday

Ted Pease

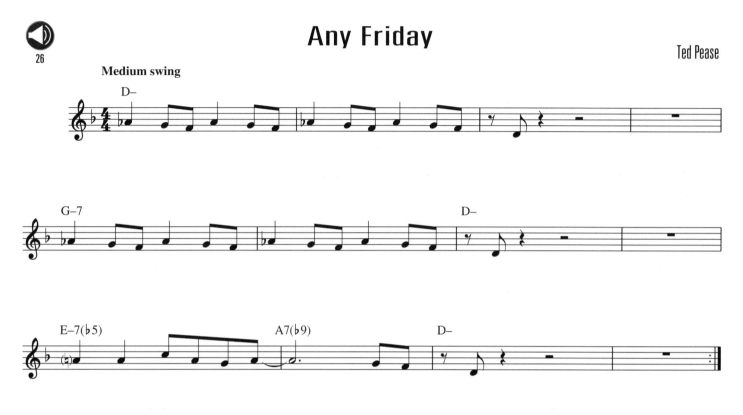

The *abc* (through-composed) type of blues contains no phrase repetition. In other words, there are no riffs as in *aaa* or *aab* blues tunes, just one continuous melodic line. Through-composed blues are usually instrumental. "Blues for Alice" (Charlie Parker) and "Au Privave" (Charlie Parker) are good examples.

***abc* (through-composed):** Major key, using the F blues scale

Blues for a Bilious Bystander

Ted Pease

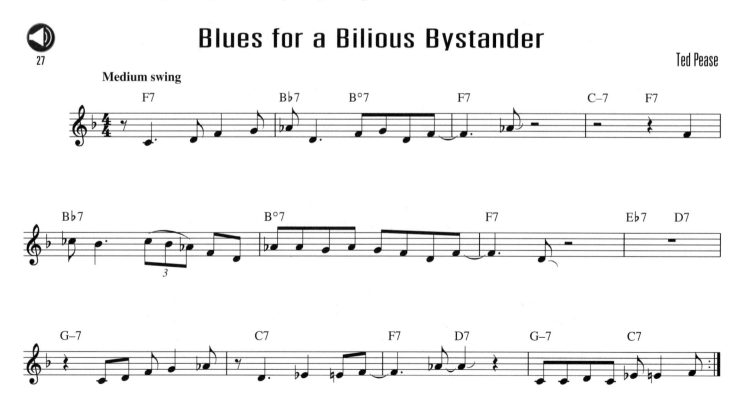

abc (**bebop**): Major key

Move It

Ted Pease

abc: Modal

Strong Currents

Ted Pease

abc (**contemporary**): Symmetric diminished scale

Blues melodies make heavy use of the blues scale whether in major, minor, or modal contexts. Early blues styles use simple melodic rhythms that are easily memorized. Bebop blues melodies have a more dense melodic rhythm and a potential increase in chromaticism (notes outside the key). Modal blues melodies tend to be diatonic to the mode, but there may be some non-diatonic notes if modal interchange is used in the harmony.

The blues scale can take several other forms. The simplest blues scale is a minor pentatonic scale.

This scale is particularly useful for novice writers and players because any and all of the notes can be used freely, regardless of where one is in the progression.

EXERCISES

Write original blues melodies for the following sets of changes. Be sure to observe tempo and style. Use the examples on the previous pages as a guide.

(a) *aaa* **(riff-type)**

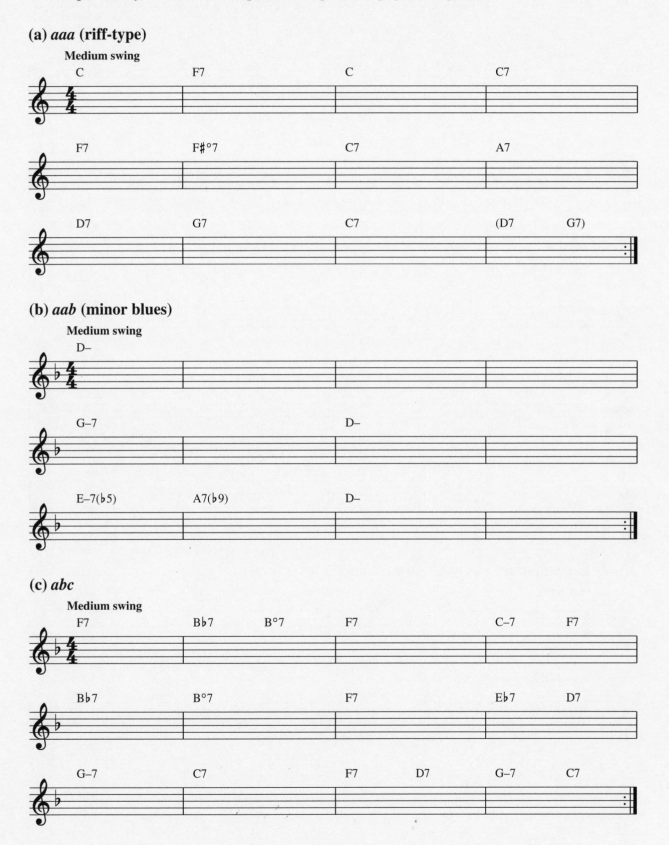

(b) *aab* **(minor blues)**

(c) *abc*

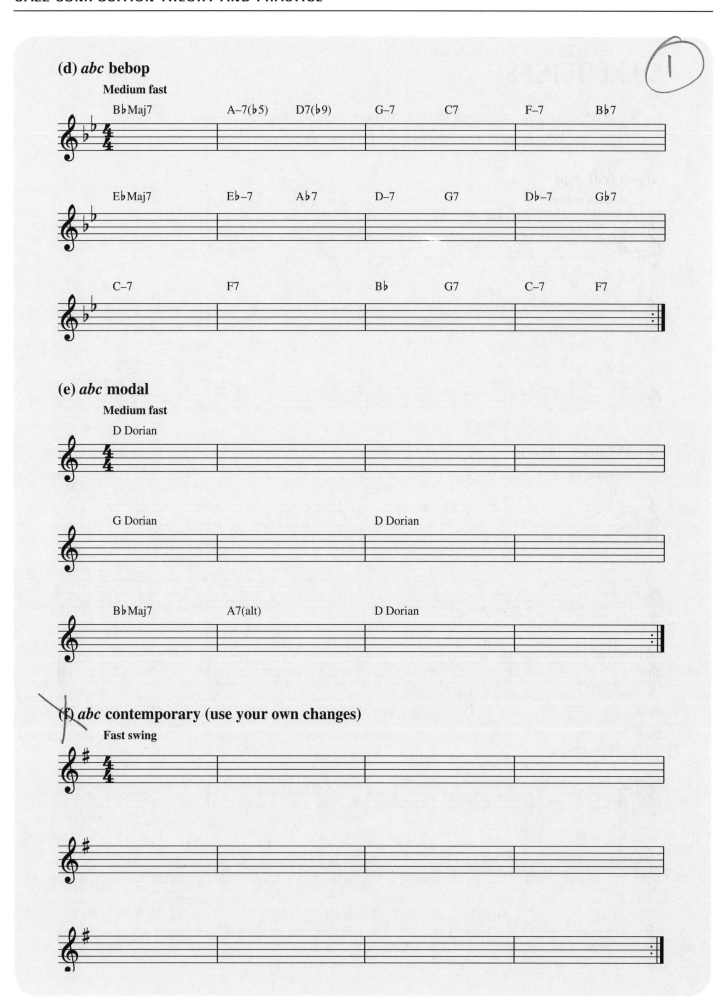

(d) *abc* **bebop**

Medium fast

B♭Maj7 | A–7(♭5) | D7(♭9) | G–7 | C7 | F–7 | B♭7

E♭Maj7 | E♭–7 | A♭7 | D–7 | G7 | D♭–7 | G♭7

C–7 | F7 | B♭ | G7 | C–7 | F7

(e) *abc* **modal**

Medium fast

D Dorian

G Dorian | D Dorian

B♭Maj7 | A7(alt) | D Dorian

(f) *abc* **contemporary (use your own changes)**

Fast swing

Additional Blues Exercises

1. Write an original 12-measure blues in C major using *aab* melodic form.

2. Write an original 12-measure blues in G minor using *aaa* melodic form and using the G minor pentatonic scale.

3. Write an original 12-measure through-composed blues in F major.

4. Write an original 24-measure blues in A minor and in 3/4 time.

5. Write an original 16-measure blues in G major.

6. Write an original 12-measure blues in D Dorian.

7. Write an original 12-measure blues in E Phrygian.

8. Write an original 12-measure blues in A♭ Mixolydian.

Source Material—Blues

Au Privave (Charles Parker)
All Blues (Miles Davis): modal blues
Bags' Groove (Milt Jackson)
Bass Blues (John Coltrane)
Bessie's Blues (John Coltrane)
Birk's Works (Dizzy Gillespie): minor blues
Blues Connotation (Ornette Coleman)
Blues for Alice (Charlie Parker)
Blues for Yna Yna (Gerald Wilson): 24-measure minor blues in 3/4
Canteloupe Island (Herbie Hancock): blues form with reharmonized changes
C Jam Blues–aka Duke's Place (Duke Ellington)
Doodlin' (Horace Silver)
Eighty-one (Ron Carter)
Filthy McNasty (Horace Silver): with written intro, out chorus, and coda
Footprints (Wayne Shorter): in 6/4
Honky Tonk Train Blues (Meade Lux Lewis)
Interplay (Bill Evans): minor blues
The Intimacy of the Blues (Billy Strayhorn)
Isotope (Joe Henderson)
Mamacita (Joe Henderson)
Moon Germs (Joe Farrell)
Mr. P.C. (John Coltrane)
Nutville (Horace Silver): 24-measure minor blues with an ostinato
Opus de Funk (Horace Silver)
Pursuance (John Coltrane): modal blues
Roll 'em Pete (Pete Johnson)
Sandu (Clifford Brown)
Sing Me Softly of the Blues (Carla Bley): non-traditional 14-measure form
Some Other Blues (John Coltrane)
Sonny Moon for Two (Sonny Rollins)
St. Louis Blues (W.C. Handy)
Things Ain't What They Used to Be (Mercer Ellington)
T.N.T. (Tiny Kahn): *a-b-a; b-a-b* melodic form over two choruses
Unit Seven (Sam Jones): blues with a bridge
Watermelon Man (Herbie Hancock): 16-measure blues with an ostinato
West Coast Blues (Wes Montgomery)
When Will the Blues Leave? (Ornette Coleman)
Windflower (Sarah Cassey): modal blues
Witch Hunt (Wayne Shorter): 24-measure blues

Rhythm Changes

"I Got Rhythm" is a show tune written by George Gershwin, with lyrics by his brother Ira, for their 1930 musical *Girl Crazy.* Next to the blues, so-called "rhythm changes" are the second most popular form that jazz musicians like to jam on. Because of the popularity of this harmonic form, numerous jazz tunes that follow rhythm changes are, in effect, recompositions of "I Got Rhythm." Below are some representative titles and composers in rough chronological order.

> Cottontail (Duke Ellington)
> Lester Leaps In (Lester Young)
> Anthropology (Charlie Parker)
> Shawnuff (Dizzy Gillespie and Charlie Parker)
> Rhythm-a-ning (Thelonious Monk)
> Oleo (Sonny Rollins)
> Fingers (Thad Jones)
> Brown Zone (Steve Khan/Yellowjackets)
> Bite Your Grandmother (Steve Swallow)

The Gershwin brothers' "I Got Rhythm" is a 34-measure tune in *aaba* form with a tag ending. Jazz composers and performers tend to leave out the tag ending, thereby retaining the familiarity of a symmetric 32-measure song form. Today, rhythm changes are essentially the same as they were in the 1930s, although numerous substitute chords are often employed by arrangers and by alert improvisers. (See "Variations on Rhythm Changes," page 130.)

Observe the following tune, "Scooter," which is based on rhythm changes and written in the swing style of the late 1930s. The first four measures are based on the familiar I VI II V chord pattern. Measures 5 and 6 are based on another familiar chord pattern: I V7/IV IV IV–. This well-known progression produces a strong counterline, which can be used against the melody, either in the bass or in an interior part:

The first ending contains a "turnaround," which gets you back to the beginning (as you go around for the second *a* phrase). The second ending contains a firm cadence.

The *b* section (known as the "bridge," the "release," or the "channel") contains four dominant seventh chords that begin on III7 (D7 in the key of B♭). D7 then moves to G7, which in turn moves to C7 and then to F7 before returning via Da Capo (D.C.) to the top. This progression is often described as "dominant chords in a cycle of fifths." It presents an ideal situation for a melodic sequence. Compare measures 11–14 with measures 15–18 and you will see how nicely a four-measure sequence works here.

After the bridge, the *a* section is played one more time, and the coda (or, if preferred, a third ending) finishes off one chorus of the tune in *aaba* form. (A full discussion of *aaba* form begins on page 132.)

Scooter

Ted Pease

"Thad's Pad" (dedicated to Thad Jones) is also based on rhythm changes, but the melody of the tune is through-composed. Each eight-measure phrase has a different melody. In other words, the form of the melody is *abcd*, while the form of the changes is still *aaba*. Unlike through-composed blues tunes, which are quite common, through-composed rhythm tunes are relatively rare.

Thad's Pad

Ted Pease

VARIATIONS ON RHYTHM CHANGES

There are almost as many variations on rhythm changes as there are on blues changes. Here are a few of them.

measures 1–4

1. B♭	G–7	C–7	F7	D–7	G–7	C–7	F7	
2. B♭	B°7	C–7	F7	B♭	B°7	C–7	F7	
3. B♭ pedal		⁒		⁒		⁒		
4. B♭	B♭7	E♭	E♭–	B♭/F pedal		C–7	F7	
5. F♯–7	B7	E–7	A7	D–7	G7	C–7	F7	
6. B♭	G7	C7	C♭7	B♭	G7	G♭7	F7	

measures 5–8

				1.				2. 3.		
1. B♭	B♭7	E♭	E♭–	D–7 G7	C–7	F7 :	‖ B♭	F7	B♭	‖
2. B♭	B♭7/D	E♭	E°7	B♭/F G7	C–7	F7 :	B♭	F7	B♭	
3. F–7	B♭7	E♭–7	A♭7	D–7 G7	C–7	F7 :	B♭	F7	B♭	
4. B♭	B♭7	E♭	E♭–	B♭ F7	B♭	:	B♭	F7	B♭	
5. B♭	B♭7/D	E♭	E°7	B♭/F pedal	⁒	:	B♭	F7	B♭	
6. F–7	B♭7	E♭	A♭7	B♭ G7	G♭7	F7 :	‖ B♭	F7	B♭	‖

bridge measures 1–4

1. D7		⁒		G7		⁒	
2. A–7		D7		D–7		G7	
3. D7		⁒		D♭7		⁒	
4. A–7		D7		D–7		G7	
5. E♭–7		A♭7		A♭–7		D♭7	
6. D7	E–7	F°7	D7/F♯	G7	A–7	B♭°7	G7/B

bridge measures 5–8

D.C. al 3rd ending

1. C7		⁒		F7		⁒	
2. G–7		C7		C–7		F7	
3. C7		⁒		B7		⁒	
4. F♯–7	B7	E–7	A7	D–7	G7	C–7	F7
5. D♭–7		G♭7		G♭–7		C♭7	
6. C7	D–7	E♭°7	C7/E	F7	G–7	A♭°7	F7/A

EXERCISE

Write a tune based on rhythm changes. Use "Scooter" and the rhythm changes template as a guide. Use appropriate substitutions and/or reharmonizations if you wish. In the *a* section, use a four-measure antecedent phrase followed by a four-measure consequent phrase that contains a "turnaround" in the first ending to get you back to the top. The second time through the *a* section, finish the consequent phrase with a musical "period." The bridge (the *b* section) is perfectly suited for sequences of two measures or four measures because of the dominant seventh chords that move in a cycle of fifths. Supply a coda (or a third ending) to show how the tune should end.

Rhythm Changes Template

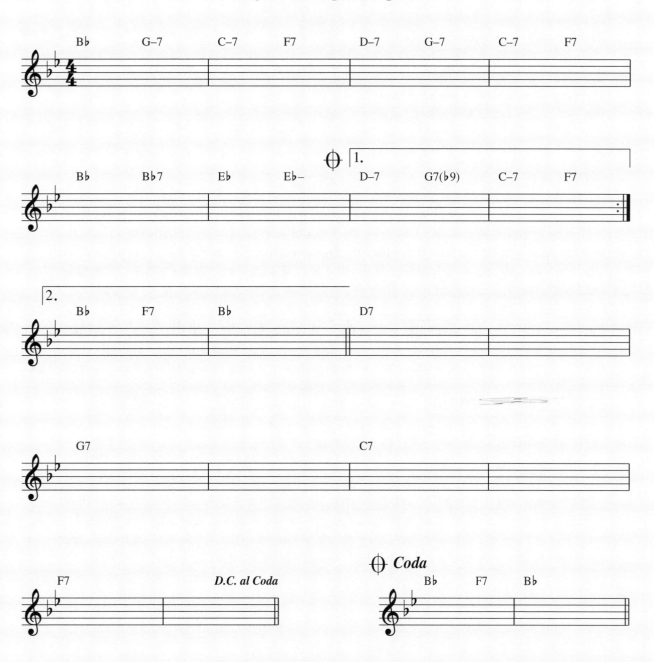

Source Material—Rhythm Changes

Anthropology (Charlie Parker)
Bird Food (Ornette Coleman)
Bite Your Grandmother (Steve Swallow)
Brown Zone (Steve Khan)
Chasing the Bird (Charlie Parker)
Cottontail (Duke Ellington)
Fingers (Thad Jones)
Four Others (Lighthouse) (Jimmy Giuffre)
Lester Leaps In (Lester Young)
Little Pixie (Thad Jones)
Moose the Mooche (Charlie Parker)
Oleo (Sonny Rollins)
Red Cross (Charlie Parker)
Rhythm-a-ning (Thelonious Monk)
Shawnuff (Charlie Parker/Dizzy Gillespie)
Steeplechase (Charlie Parker)
Thriving from a Riff (Charlie Parker)
Wee — aka Allen's Alley (Denzil Best)

aaba Form

As we have seen, rhythm changes are based on *aaba* form. (I am using lowercase letters to designate *aaba* song form. Later, we will examine extended compositions in which an *aaba* song might be a subsection of a longer A section or B section of a movement, for which uppercase letters will be used). By the way, Beethoven's "Ode to Joy," which is used numerous times in the book for demonstration purposes, is also in *aaba* form!

Supplied with "rhythm changes," you wrote an original melody on that form. Now it is time to try writing an original melody *and* original harmony. A word of caution! At this point, many students will write a chord progression and then compose a melody over it. This can work, as we have seen with rhythm changes and the blues, but there is always the potential problem that the harmony will end up dictating the melody. Ideally, it should be the other way around. I suspect that the Gershwin brothers came up with the melody for the title lyric of "I Got Rhythm" first and then put a simple I VI II V progression under it.

The problem with writing the chord progression first is that later you may find yourself puzzling over what chord scales you should use for the melody, and whether you are breaking any "rules." This, in turn, may result in what I call a "tortured" melody, which is a melody that you arrive at mechanically rather than aurally (by ear).

Now would be a good time to review Chapter 1 of this book. As you begin to think about the melody for your original *aaba* tune, start with some questions: What is the first melodic interval of my tune going to be? Will it be a repeated note? A second? A fifth? An octave? What will the next interval be? What is the first rhythm going to be? And *then*, before you ask yourself any more questions, *Sing something!* A short lick, a scalewise passage, an interval, a rhythm—anything. If it clicks, jot it down. Then play it on your instrument. Then ask yourself, "Okay, what happens next?"

Hopefully, by now, you have the beginnings of a four-measure antecedent phrase. If the first lick is two measures long and you like it, try repeating it. Or try a sequence (up a major second often works well). Or if the first lick moves up, move the second lick down. Keep singing and keep playing.

If you are happy with the antecedent phrase, you can choose whether to complete the consequent phrase or to put some chord changes to the antecedent phrase. Review the related text for ideas. In most cases, a consequent phrase should end with a turnaround the first time (to get you back to the top), and a full cadence the second time with a pivot chord to get you into the bridge. If you are choosing chords, experiment with different levels of tension on the first few notes of your melody and see what that suggests for subsequent chords.

The bridge (the *b* section) of an *aaba* tune should present a new idea that provides contrast with the *a* section. There is also the possibility of modulating to a new key. Following is a short list of *a* section/bridge key relationships from representative jazz tunes.

Tune	Composer	*a* section ending key	*b* section starting key
Satin Doll	Duke Ellington	C	F
In a Sentimental Mood	Duke Ellington	F	D♭
Prelude to a Kiss	Duke Ellington	C	E
Daahoud	Clifford Brown	E♭	A♭
Jeannine	Duke Pearson	A♭	D♭
Morning	Clare Fischer	B♭−	D♭
Pensativa	Clare Fischer	G♭	C
If You Could See Me Now	Tadd Dameron	E♭	G

Below is a partial list that suggests other tonal and modal relationships:

If the *a* section ends in:	try modulating in the bridge to:
I major (e.g., C major)	relative minor (e.g., A minor)
I major (e.g., C major)	parallel minor (e.g., C minor)
I major (e.g., C major)	IV major (e.g., F major)
I major (e.g., C major)	VI major (e.g., A major)
I major (e.g., C major)	♭II major (e.g., D♭ major)
I major (e.g., C major)	♭VI major (e.g., A♭ major)
I minor (e.g., C minor)	relative major (e.g., E♭ major)
I minor (e.g., C minor)	parallel major (e.g., C major)
I minor (e.g., C minor)	IV minor (e.g., F minor)
I Dorian (e.g., D Dorian)	♭II Dorian (e.g., E♭ Dorian)
I Phrygian (e.g., E Phrygian)	IV major (e.g., A major)

Observe the next two tunes, "Rascals" and "Your Smile." In "Rascals," the *a* section is in A Dorian. The melody is diatonic and contains simple melodic rhythms with 1 and 5 of the mode emphasized with long notes. The characteristic note (F♯) occurs in measure 6 and helps us to identify the mode as Dorian rather than Aeolian. The *b* section contains a two-measure "riff" that moves up in half steps (sequence!) to a concluding percussive figure in measure 15.

Rascals

Ted Pease

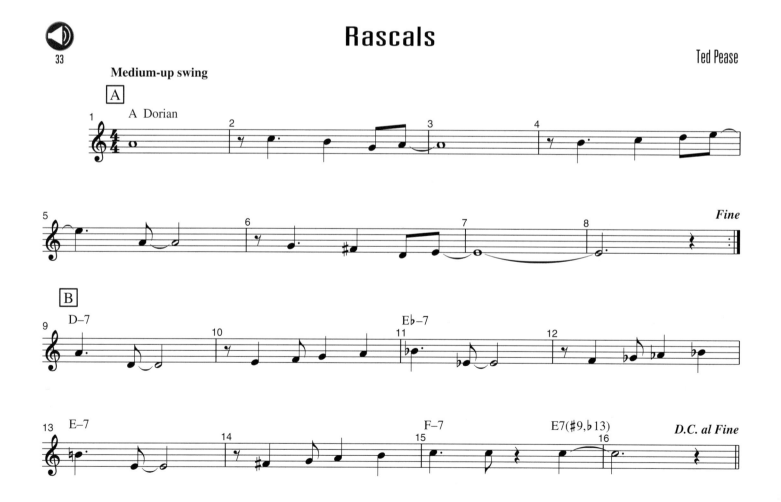

"Your Smile" is a ballad in D♭ major. The *a* section antecedent phrase utilizes a melodic sequence. The consequent phrase continues the sequence downwards in measure 5 but moves back up in measure 6. The first ending contains a melodic cadence to 3 of the key on a D♭Maj7 chord and the turnaround chord, B♭7. The second ending contains a melodic cadence to the tonic of the key on D♭6/9. The bridge contains an antecedent phrase in G♭ (IV major of D♭) and a consequent phrase in B♭ (VI major of D♭) with chords in measure 18 to get us back to the beginning. The last *a* section has a different consequent phrase that contains the apex of the tune in measure 20. Accordingly, we should label the form *aaba'* (note the apostrophe), and speak of it as "*aab-a* 'prime'" (The term "prime" is used to designate a slight melodic or harmonic deviation from an earlier related *a* section, but one that leaves the essence of the *a* section intact. The "prime" designation is used most commonly when a consequent phrase is different, as is the case with "Your Smile." Simple deviations in a first and second ending are usually not cause for using the "prime" designation.)

Your Smile

Ted Pease

WARM-UP EXERCISE

Following is a template for a tune in *aaba* form. The changes and a suggested rhythm are supplied. Write an *a* section in D Dorian using the given rhythm for the melody (notice that the *a* section repeats). Write a *b* section using the given chord changes and the suggested rhythm. Then write the *a* section again.

EXERCISES

1. Write an original 32-measure tune in *aaba* form. Choose a major key, the tempo, and the style. Go to the key of IV in the bridge. Include a prominent melodic rhythm in the *a* section to serve as a musical fingerprint. (Review pages 4–9.)

2. Write a 32-measure bossa nova in *aaba* form. Put the *a* sections in D minor and the *b* section in F major. Use at least one prominent melodic rhythm.

3. Write a 32-measure jazz waltz in *aaba* form. Put the *a* sections in B♭ major and the *b* section in G minor.

4. Write a ballad in E♭ major in *aaba* form. Make the *a* sections four measures long and the *b* section eight measures long. Use a pedal point in the *a* sections. Go to A♭ major in the *b* section.

5. Write a 32-measure tune in *aaba* form. Put the *a* sections in A minor with a Latin feel. Put the *b* section in C major with a swing feel.

6. Write a 32-measure tune in *aaba'* form. Put the *a* sections in E Phrygian and the *b* section in B♭ Lydian. In the final *a'* (*a* "prime") section, use a slight melodic and/or harmonic deviation from the previous *a* sections.

7. Write a tune in *aaba* form in which the bridge is in blues form.

8. Write an *aaba* tune in which the *a* sections are in blues form but the bridge is not.

Source Material—*aaba* form

Note: Deviations from standard 32-measure form are noted inside brackets [ ]. You will also find the apostrophe (') and the double apostrophe ("), which are used to indicate that despite a noticeable alteration in the melody and/or the harmony, the basic essence of a preceding *a* or *b* section is still present. (See "Tell Me A Bedtime Story" below.)

Aisha (McCoy Tyner) [ostinato in the *a* section]
Bernie's Tune (Bernie Miller)
Black Nile (Wayne Shorter) [*aa'ba*]
The Blessing (Ornette Coleman)
Blue Spirits (Freddie Hubbard) [16–16–16–16 in 3/4]
Boplicity (Miles Davis)
Bouncin' with Bud (Bud Powell) [*aa'ba* with an eight-measure tag]
Cassidae (John Scofield) [*aabba* (16–16–7–7–16)]
Chelsea Bridge (Billy Strayhorn)
Come Sunday (Duke Ellington)
Daahoud (Clifford Brown)
Day Dream (Duke Ellington/Billy Strayhorn)
Don't Let It Go (Vincent Herring)
The Duke (Dave Brubeck) [*aaba* with a final coda]
Four Brothers (Jimmy Giuffre)
Gee Baby, Ain't I Good to You (Don Redman)[4–4–4–4]
Grand Central (John Coltrane) [*aaba'* (8–8–8–12)]
Honeysuckle Rose (Fats Waller)
Impressions (John Coltrane)
If You Could See Me Now (Tadd Dameron)
I Mean You (Thelonious Monk) [8–8–8–8–tag]
I Remember August (Ralph Towner)
In a Sentimental Mood (Duke Ellington)
In Walked Bud (Thelonious Monk)
Jacqui (Richie Powell) [8–8–12–8; bridge is in blues form]
Jeannine (Duke Pearson)
Jordu (Duke Jordan)

Killer Joe (Benny Golson)
Lester Left Town (Wayne Shorter) [16–16–16–16]
Line for Lyons (Gerry Mulligan)
Little Sunflower (Freddie Hubbard) [*aabbaa*]
Loco Motiv (Larry Gales) [22–22–8–22]
Maiden Voyage (Herbie Hancock)
Monk's Mood (Thelonious Monk)
Morning (Clare Fischer)
Naima (John Coltrane) [4–4–8–4]
Nica's Dream (Horace Silver) [16–16–16-16–tag]
One by One (Wayne Shorter)
Pensativa (Clare Fischer) [16–16–16–16]
Pent Up House (Sonny Rollins) [4–4–4–4]
Prelude to a Kiss (Duke Ellington)
Satin Doll (Duke Ellington/Billy Strayhorn)
Seven Steps to Heaven (Victor Feldman) [8–8–8–8 with an interlude between solos]
Solitude (Duke Ellington)
Song for My Father (Horace Silver)
Sophisticated Lady (Duke Ellington)
So What (Miles Davis)
Speak No Evil (Wayne Shorter) [14–14–8–14]
Stablemates (Benny Golson) [*aba* (14–8–14)]
Straight Street (John Coltrane) [12–12–12–12]
Tell Me a Bedtime Story (Herbie Hancock) [*aa'ba"* (12–12–8–12)]
This Is for Albert (Wayne Shorter)
Toy Tune (Wayne Shorter) [8–8–4–8]
Unit Seven (Sam Jones) [blues with a bridge]
Up Jumped Spring (Freddie Hubbard) [16–16–8–16 in 3/4]
Wabash III (John Scofield)
Well You Needn't (Thelonious Monk)
Whisper Not (Benny Golson) [with written out-chorus]
Woody'n You (Dizzy Gillespie)
Yes and No (Wayne Shorter) [14–14–16–14]
Yesterday and Today (Dario Eskenazi) [16–16–16–18 plus an interlude]

abac Form

The *abac* form presents an excellent opportunity to use longer antecedent and consequent phrase lengths. Instead of four-measure antecedent and consequent phrases, which are common in *aaba* form, eight-measure phrases may provide better overall balance and also keep *abac* form from becoming too cluttered.

With *abac* form, there are only two *a* sections (as compared to three with *aaba* form). Furthermore, there are two other sections that can provide necessary contrast (the *b* section and the *c* section). This makes it possible to consider the entire *a* section as an antecedent phrase, and the entire *b* section as a consequent phrase. At that point, the *a* section (the eight-measure antecedent phrase) repeats. Then the *c* section provides yet another eight-measure consequent phrase to complete the form:

> *a* antecedent (8)—one element
> *b* consequent (8)—a contrasting element
> *a* antecedent (8)—the original element
> *c* consequent (8)—a different contrasting element
> Total of different elements in the tune as a whole: three

Remember, antecedent and consequent phrases are grammatical phrases—that is, elements of musical conversation. Just as in spoken language, their overall length can be subdivided into breathing phrases for performance purposes without sacrificing the grammatical content.

In comparison, *aaba* form contains three *a* sections. There is a greater need for contrast within each *a* section so that a tune doesn't become too repetitive. This contrast is provided by an antecedent phrase and a consequent phrase in each *a* section, as well as a new antecedent phrase and a new consequent phrase in the bridge:

> *a* antecedent (4), consequent (4)—two elements
> *a* antecedent (4), consequent (4)—the same two elements
> *b* new antecedent (4), new consequent (4)—two new elements
> *a* antecedent (4), consequent (4)—the original two elements
> Total of different elements in the tune as a whole: four

Further contrast within *aaba* form is provided (in most tunes) by a temporary modulation to a new key in the bridge.

There is another, more subtle result that occurs with *abac* form. It is possible to consider the entire first half of the form (*ab*) as an even larger antecedent element and the entire second half (*ac*) as a balancing consequent element.

The term "phrase" begins to lose its meaning when we speak of structural elements longer than eight measures. The term "period" might be more appropriate. Period is a common term used in classical music to describe a musical statement consisting of two phrases. However, jazz musicians rarely use the term. They are more liable to say things like, "The first half of the tune does so-and-so, and the second half does such-and-such."

Most *abac* tunes contain a primary apex, or climax, in the *c* section. This provides additional reinforcement of the form through a natural crescendo as the tune progresses. Observe the following tune, "For Bill" (dedicated to Bill Evans). The primary apex occurs in the fourth measure of the second ending.

For Bill

Ted Pease

Refer back to "Diminishing Returns" (page 35, audio track 5) for a tune in *abac* form that contains asymmetric phrasing. The *a* section contains twelve measures, the *b* section (first ending) contains sixteen measures, and the *c* section (second ending) contains twenty measures. The primary apex occurs in measure 34 (the sixth measure of the second ending.)

EXERCISES

1. Write a 32-measure tune in F major in *abac* form. Use a distinctive melodic rhythm in the *a* section. Use a different melodic rhythm in the *b* section and a similar melodic rhythm in the *c* section. Use sequences freely. Place the climax of the tune in the *c* section.

2. Write a 32-measure jazz waltz in *abac* form. Use eight-measure antecedent and consequent phrases.

3. Write a 64-measure jazz samba in *abac* form. Use sixteen-measure antecedent and consequent phrases.

4. Write a 32-measure tune in *abac* form. Use a Latin feel in the *a* sections and swing in the *b* and *c* sections.

Source Material—*abac* form

Deviations from standard 32-measure form are noted.

A Child Is Born (Thad Jones)
Airegin (Sonny Rollins) [8–12–8–8]
All Across the City (Jim Hall)
Another Time (Alan Broadbent) [8–8–8–10]
Ceora (Lee Morgan)
Dig (Miles Davis)
Donna Lee (Charles Parker) [*aba'c*]
Epiphany (Denny Zeitlin)
Four (Miles Davis)
In a Mellow Tone (Duke Ellington)
Isfahan (Duke Ellington/Billy Strayhorn)
It's Only Music (Gary Willis)
Lament (J.J. Johnson)
Moment's Notice (John Coltrane) [with written intro; form is 8–8–8–14 including tag]
Morning of the Carnival (Luiz Bonfa)
New Girl (Duke Pearson) [8–4–8–8]
Quasimodo (Charlie Parker)
Soul Eyes (Mal Waldron)
Strollin' (Horace Silver)
Teaneck (Nat Adderley)

Ostinatos (Revisited)

Ever since Dizzy Gillespie and others began incorporating Latin rhythms in some of their tunes in the 1940s, jazz composers have used ostinatos as a means of highlighting bass lines and achieving textural and stylistic contrast in their work. The influence of rock music and fusion in the 1960s and 1970s reinforced the importance of the bass, thanks in part to the contributions of virtuoso electric bass players such as Jaco Pastorius, Stanley Clarke, and Abraham Laboriel.

A number of jazz standards feature ostinatos:

> A Night in Tunisia (Dizzy Gillespie)
> Manteca (Dizzy Gillespie and Chano Pozo)
> Take Five (Paul Desmond)
> All Blues (Miles Davis)
> So What (Miles Davis)
> Killer Joe (Benny Golson)
> Watermelon Man (Herbie Hancock)
> Maiden Voyage (Herbie Hancock)
> Footprints (Wayne Shorter)
> Chameleon (Herbie Hancock)
> Red Clay (Freddie Hubbard)
> Rosewood (Woody Shaw)
> Birdland (Joe Zawinul)

Ostinatos are repetitive rhythmic and melodic patterns in the bass. Observe "Sez Who?" on the next page and listen to it on the audio. Notice that the ostinato is established in the introduction before the melody enters. This is typical of tunes with ostinatos. (Sometimes the bass will start, followed by the keyboard the second time, and the drums the third time. This is called "layering.") Notice also that the ostinato has a harmonic sequence in the third and fourth measures (up a major 2nd from the first and second measures).

Notice that there is a lot of space in the melody in measures 1, 3, 4, 9, 11, and 12. This gives the rhythm section a chance to be in the foreground and to enhance the groove.

In the *b* section, notice the A–7 chords. These are modal interchange chords from G major, the parallel major. They are used to avoid the diatonic tritone (B♭ to E) in G Dorian. This particular progression is one of Oliver Nelson's trademarks in tunes like "Stolen Moments."

Sez Who?

Ted Pease

EXERCISES

1. Write an *abac* tune on the staves provided below using an ostinato in the *a* sections and straight time in the *b* and *c* sections.

2. Research the tunes that use ostinatos listed on page 143. Find lead sheets and recordings wherever possible.

Source Material—Ostinatos

Aisha (McCoy Tyner)
All Blues (Miles Davis)
Afro-Centric (Joe Henderson)
Birdland (Joe Zawinul)
Bolivia (Cedar Walton)
Black Narcissus (Joe Henderson)
Canteloupe Island (Herbie Hancock)
Chameleon (Herbie Hancock)
Fly with the Wind (McCoy Tyner)
Footprints (Wayne Shorter)
Killer Joe (Benny Golson)
Little Sunflower (Freddie Hubbard)
Loco Motiv (Larry Gales)
Maiden Voyage (Herbie Hancock)
Mamacita (Joe Henderson)
Manteca (Dizzy Gillespie and Chano Pozo)
Memory and Desire (Billy Childs)
Naima (John Coltrane)
A Night in Tunisia (Dizzy Gillespie)
Nutville (Horace Silver)
Paladia (Steve Masakowski)
Red Clay (Freddie Hubbard)
Rosewood (Woody Shaw)
Song for My Father (Horace Silver)
So What (Miles Davis)
Take Five (Paul Desmond)
Watermelon Man (Herbie Hancock)

abca Song Form

The *abca* song form is relatively rare. The most well-known standard written in this form is "Stella by Starlight" by Victor Young. The *a*, *b*, and *c* sections of the form are through-composed in a continuously building manner so that the apex (climax) is reached in the *c* section. The concluding *a* section (actually *a'* since the consequent phrase is different than the one in the first *a* section) is like a postscript—a return to relative calm in a lower register.

Study the following tune, "Scrooge." Notice how the tune builds toward the climax in measure 21. Measures 5–6 are a sequence of measures 1–2. Measures 9, 11, and 13 demonstrate melodic sequence. Measures 17 and 19 demonstrate an inversion of the melodic line in measures 9, 11, and 13. Measure 19 is a sequence of measure 17.

Scrooge

Ted Pease

EXERCISE

Write a tune in *abca* form using "Scrooge" as a model. Use a distinctive melodic rhythm as you develop the tune. Use sequences freely. Place the climax in the *c* section.

Through-Composed Tunes

A through-composed tune derives its unity from motivic repetition and development rather than from phrase repetition. Thus, a through-composed tune is one with a continually evolving melody. Its form can be described as *abcd...* instead of *aaba* or *abac*.

Motivic manipulation is the key to success in a through-composed tune. You need a short melodic fragment (an interval, a rhythmic figure, a melodic gesture) that will still be recognizable even when it is partially disguised. That motif can be repeated, sequenced, inverted, played backward, transformed pitch-wise or rhythmically, and in general manipulated imaginatively to produce the variety necessary to sustain interest.

Some of these melodic devices are demonstrated below, using excerpts from the next tune, "Samba de Goofed."

The principal motif is:

The principal motif is altered rhythmically and intervallically to produce the following variation:

These two melodic and rhythmic fragments provide the main focus for the tune.

Motivic repetition
Motivic repetition is demonstrated in measures 17 and 19, and again in measures 21 and 23.

Motivic sequence

Motivic sequence is demonstrated in a comparison of measures 1–2 with measures 5–6.

Motivic sequence occurs again in a comparison of measures 17–20 with measures 21–24.

becomes

Motivic sequence occurs again in a comparison of measures 33–34 with measures 35–36.

Motivic displacement

Motivic displacement occurs in a comparison of measure 1 with measure 3.

Motivic transformation: same rhythm, different pitches

Motivic transformation occurs throughout the tune. As the motif is manipulated, the rhythm remains the same but the pitch keeps changing.

Motivic transformation: same pitches, different rhythm

In measures 1 and 3 the pitches remain the same but the rhythm changes through displacement.

Motivic embellishment

Motivic embellishment occurs in measure 27.

Tonal inversion

Inversion changes the direction of a melodic gesture from up to down, or from down to up. Tonal inversion adjusts the intervals either to leave the tonality undisturbed or to create a wider or narrower interval in the inversion. Exact inversion maintains the exact intervallic relationships even if the tonality is disturbed in the process. Tonal inversion occurs in a comparison of measures 1 and 9. The perfect fourth in measure 1 inverts to a perfect fifth in measure 9. The melodic gesture changes from downward in measure 1 to upward in measure 9. The tonality remains undisturbed.

Exact inversion

Exact inversion occurs in a comparison of measures 6 and 14. The consecutive intervals of a major second, a minor second, and a major third in measure 6 are mirrored in measure 14. (As it turns out, this particular inversion doesn't disturb the tonality of B♭ major.)

Pitch Axis

The pitch axis refers to the line or space on the staff upon which an inverted melody rotates. The location of a pitch axis is at the discretion of the composer. Below are some examples of a melody that has been inverted on several different pitch axes. (Note: The resulting inversion can be used in any octave.)

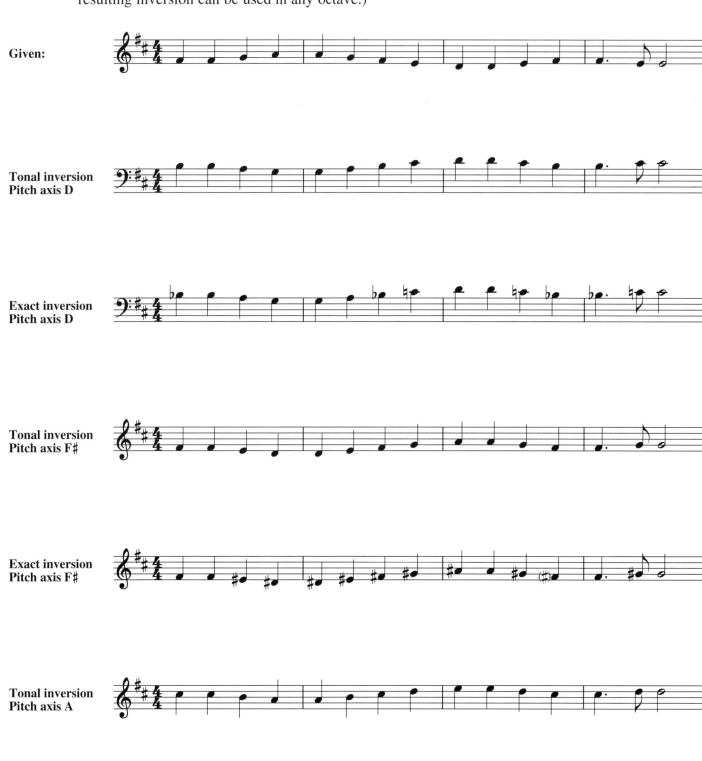

Given:

Tonal inversion Pitch axis D

Exact inversion Pitch axis D

Tonal inversion Pitch axis F♯

Exact inversion Pitch axis F♯

Tonal inversion Pitch axis A

Exact inversion Pitch axis A

Retrograde (not used in "Samba de Goofed")
Retrograde position occurs when the melody is played in reverse. When exact, the retrograde is the lateral mirror image of the melody. When inexact, the retrograde mirrors the pitches, but the rhythm of the original remains the same.

Augmentation

Augmentation (the expansion of note values) occurs in a comparison of measure 33 with measures 37–38.

x = 1 = the duration of an eighth note (or an eighth-note rest)

Diminution

Diminution (the contraction of note values) occurs in measure 17.

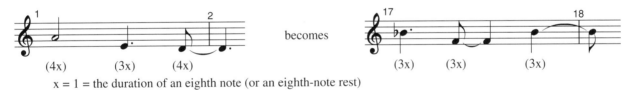

x = 1 = the duration of an eighth note (or an eighth-note rest)

Truncation

Truncation (the use of only part of the motif) is demonstrated in measure 11 and again in measure 13.

Extension

Extension (the adding of notes to the motif) is demonstrated throughout the tune when the motifs are connected by a linking figure. This happens in measures 2, 6, 10, 34, and 36.

Samba de Goofed

Ted Pease

"Where Did You Go?" is a through-composed ballad based on an ostinato and the following motifs:

The ostinato provides an additional motivic context as it alternates rhythmically with the melody:

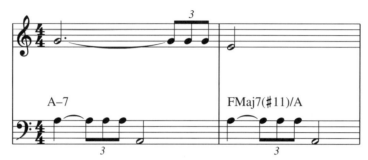

Other features of this tune include slash chords, triads over related and unrelated bass notes, and chromatic harmony that cadences only once (measure 17).

Where Did You Go?

Ted Pease

EXERCISE

Apply the designated manipulation devices to the given motifs.

EXERCISES

1. Using G as the pitch axis, demonstrate tonal inversion of the following melodic fragments.

2. Using A♭ as the pitch axis, demonstrate exact inversion of the following melodic fragments.

3. Write the following melodic fragments in inexact retrograde position (using the same forward rhythm).

4. Write the following melodic fragments in exact retrograde position (using the rhythms and pitches in reverse order).

5. Demonstrate augmentation on the following melodic fragments. Add barlines as necessary.

6. Demonstrate diminution on the following melodic fragments. Add barlines if necessary.

7. Demonstrate truncation of the following melodic fragments.

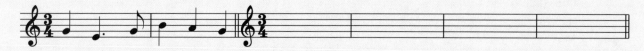

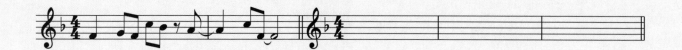

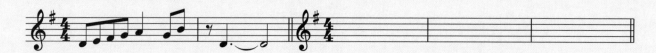

8. Demonstrate extension using the following melodic fragments.

original

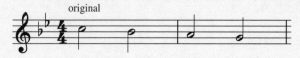

with extension

original

with extension

original

with extension

9. Write a through-composed tune.
   Write a through-composed tune of between 24 and 40 measures in length. In the process, choose a distinctive motif (an interval, melodic rhythm, or other gesture) and apply motivic manipulation as you develop the tune. You may also wish to consider the use of guide tones and their embellishments to create continuity.

Source Material—Through-Composed tunes

Blue Bossa (Kenny Dorham)
The Dolphin (Luis Eca)
Dolphin Dance (Herbie Hancock)
Falling Grace (Steve Swallow)
Giant Steps (John Coltrane)
How Insensitive (Antonio Carlos Jobim)
Humpty Dumpty (Chick Corea)
Inner Urge (Joe Henderson)
In the Woods (Phil Markowitz)
Madrid (Brad Mehldau)
Memory and Desire (Billy Childs)
One Finger Snap (Herbie Hancock)
Peace (Horace Silver)
Peri's Scope (Bill Evans)
Pinocchio (Wayne Shorter)
Time Remembered (Bill Evans)

CHAPTER 4
Arranging and Formatting Considerations

Your tunes are musical entities that can stand alone as short (but complete) compositions. However, if they are to be performed by others, arranging and formatting considerations must be addressed. Questions involving instrumentation and the size of a performing group must be answered. Will a change of key from the original be necessary? Will there be an introduction? Will there be any improvisation? Will there be interludes and/or a modulation between solos? Will there be an "arranger's chorus" in which the composition is paraphrased? How will the piece end? This chapter offers suggestions and techniques for answering these questions.

Getting Your Music Played

There is no greater incentive for further composing than hearing your own compositions played back to you. If you can play your tunes yourself, you have undoubtedly been checking your results during the composing process. But the real kick comes when you get your tunes played by and/or with other people.

If you are a piano player, perhaps a friend who plays trumpet or tenor saxophone can play the melody while you comp the changes. (Remember, your melody must be transposed up a major second from concert pitch for B♭ instruments.) If you are a guitar player, perhaps you can get a piano player to accompany you while you play your melody.

Do whatever it takes to get your music played. If you have friends or fellow students with whom you play regularly, write out your tunes for them. A simple lead sheet consisting of the melody and chord changes will do for starters. Trumpet, clarinet, soprano saxophone, and tenor saxophone require a so-called "B♭ part," which is transposed up a major second. Alto and baritone saxophone require an E♭ part, which is transposed up a major sixth and read in treble clef. Trombone requires a part in concert key written in bass clef and most likely an octave below your original lead-sheet melody.

If you wish to add some harmony parts, you may need to review a jazz arranging text for technical assistance. *Modern Jazz Voicings* by Ted Pease and Ken Pullig (book and CD published by Berklee Press) can help in that regard with a review of instrumentation, melodic and harmonic tensions, and reharmonization techniques for approach notes, as well as voicing techniques for three to six horns. Meanwhile, here are some basic guidelines for writing for two horns.

Two-Part Soli Writing

Two-part soli writing involves the use of intervals as opposed to full chords. Harmonic intervals of the second, third, fourth, fifth, sixth, and seventh are used to help define a given chord sound. Thirds and sixths are the most common choice because they are comparatively consonant intervals. Seconds, sevenths, and the tritone usually resolve immediately to thirds or sixths since they are unstable and comparatively dissonant. Fourths and fifths have an open sound that is particularly useful for modal tunes. (In jazz, parallel fourths and fifths are used freely by arrangers and composers.) Fourths and fifths are also used whenever necessary to help supply the desired chord sound.

The example below demonstrates a simple two-part harmonization (called "soli") for trumpet and tenor saxophone of a jazz version of Beethoven's "Ode to Joy" from his Ninth Symphony. I strongly recommend that you sing or play the harmony part along with the audio in order to hear how the various intervals sound and how they help to define the chord sound of the moment.

Two-part soli writing is a useful and effective technique. However, don't neglect unison and octave unison when you are writing for two horns, because those sounds, as demonstrated in measures 1, 12, 15, and 16, can be powerful, direct, and dramatic.

Ode for Two

Beethoven/arr. Pease

EXERCISES

1. Here is a lead sheet to "Rascals," the tune used earlier in the book to demonstrate *aaba* form. Add a harmony part using mostly fourths and fifths (use other intervals as necessary). When you are done, play (or sing) the harmony part along with audio (track 33).

More Rascals

Ted Pease

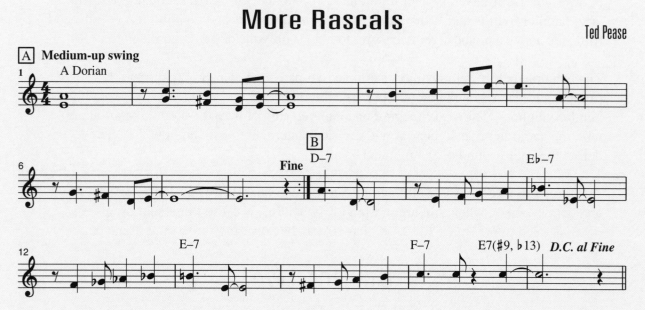

2. Here is another copy of the lead sheet to "Rascals." On this one, add a harmony part using mostly thirds and sixths (again, use other intervals as necessary). Play your harmony part along with the audio. Compare the two versions.

Even More Rascals

Ted Pease

3. Arrange one of your own tunes for two horns using the two-part soli writing technique. Copy out the horn parts, transposing for B♭ or E♭ instruments as necessary. Make copies of the lead sheet for the rhythm section. Play your arrangement.

Background Writing/
Deriving Counterpoint from Guide Tones

Guide tones are the means by which harmonic progressions can be represented linearly in a single voice. We have seen (in chapter 1) how guide tones can be used to create a melody. Guide tones can also be used to derive counterpoint and backgrounds to a melody.

Background writing involves an additional compositional process beyond the creation of the original melodic, harmonic, and rhythmic material of a piece. Backgrounds provide interesting interplay between two or more voices. This interplay is known as **counterpoint**. (The backgrounds in some jazz arrangements are as well known as the composition itself. A good example is Gil Evans' arrangement of George Gershwin's "Summertime" from *Porgy and Bess*, as performed by Miles Davis.)

Counterpoint provides relief from unison and soli textures. If you start with a melody and then add a bass line, you already have a two-part contrapuntal texture. Adding a third line based on a complementary guide tone line will provide you with a remarkably complete musical result.

The example below shows two separate guide tone lines and a bass line for a simple progression. The first example on the next page ("Small Wonder") shows how the sketch shown below might be modified with embellishments. The top guide tone line has been embellished to create a melody. The second line has been embellished to create a background to that melody. The bottom line in the bass clef has been activated to create a bass part. Notice that the melody and background are arranged in a kind of musical conversation for the first four measures. They then join forces for a more concerted soli effect in the second four measures.

Sketch

Ted Pease

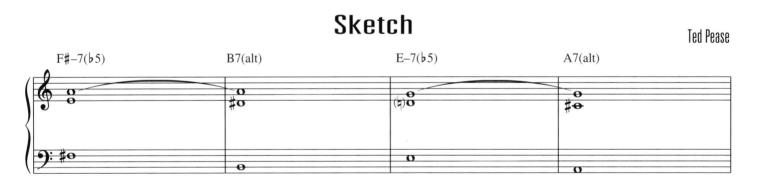

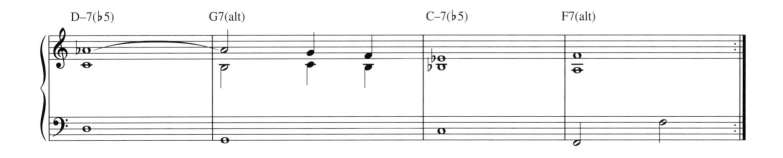

Small Wonder

Ted Pease

The following example shows how this procedure might be applied to Beethoven's "Ode to Joy."

Ode for Two Redux

Beethoven/arr. Pease

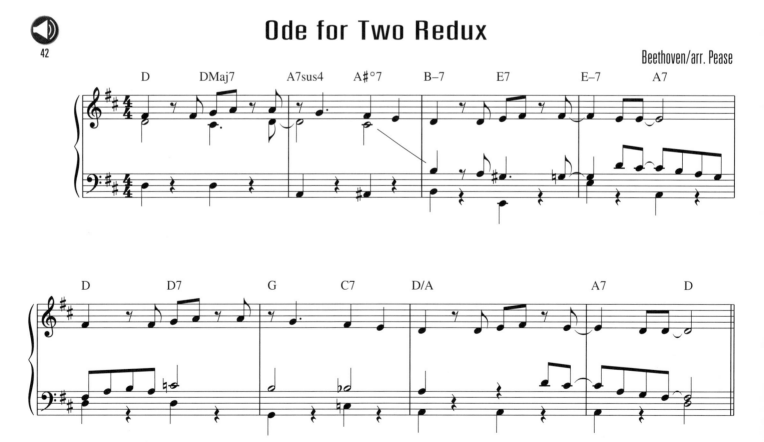

EXERCISES

1. Using page 167 as a model, construct a guide tone sketch in two parts in the treble clef based on the given chord changes. Add a sketch of the bass line in bass clef.

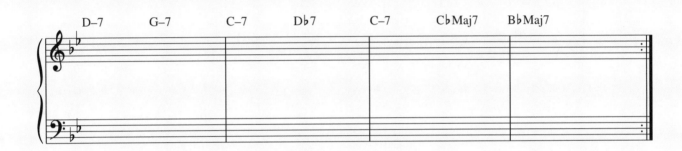

2. Now embellish the top guide tone line to create a melody. Leave some spaces for the background to fill behind the melody. Then embellish the second line and create a musical conversation. Finally, write a simple bass part.

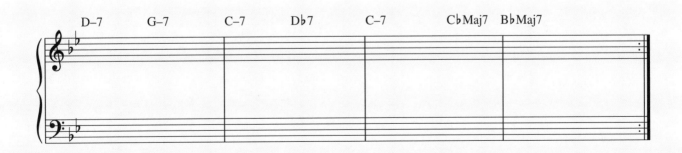

3. "And Why Not Indeed?" recalls the tune used earlier in the book to demonstrate how to write melodies using guide tones. In the exercise below, the goal is to write a background based on a complementary guide tone line. Complete the guide tone sketch on the second staff. Then embellish the sketch on the third staff to create the background. Play your background along with audio track 4.

And Why Not Indeed?

Ted Pease

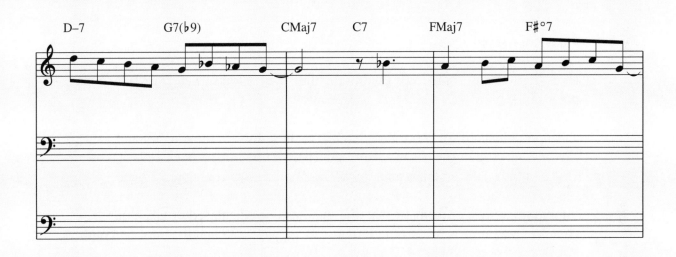

Intros, Interludes, and Endings

Intros, interludes, and endings provide additional enhancement to compositions and arrangements. Their use needs to be considered during the formatting process.

Intros (introductions) prepare the listener for what is to follow by establishing a combination of melodic, harmonic, and/or rhythmic material that relates to the main body of a piece.

Interludes provide a respite between solos or between other important sections of a piece. They can also serve as "introductions" to new internal episodes of motivic compositions and other longer works. An interlude also provides a strategic spot for a modulation.

Endings usually provide closure, or in some cases a bridge to the next movement of an extended work.

The following examples are to be found elsewhere in this book. (See also "Pedal Point" on page 92.)

Intros may consist of:

1. an ostinato that is going to be used in the tune that follows. (See "Sez Who?" on page 144.)

2. an important chord (or chord progression) that establishes the tonality and rhythmic groove of the piece. (See "And There You Are" on page 189, "Dynamic Duo" on page 208, and measures 16–19 of "Reflections" on page 229.)

3. important motivic or thematic material that has been disguised or taken out of context. (See measures 1–40 of "Initiations" on page 225 and the intro to "With All Due Respect" on page 193.)

Interludes provide a "pause" in the action. They often consist of:

1. a reference to previous motivic or thematic material accompanied by a pedal point, a broken time feel, and/or sparse chordal accompaniment. (See measures 73–78 of "Initiations" on page 226.)

2. a short bridging passage that creates a link or transition between sections of a piece. (See measures 39–42, 59–66, and 83–86 of "Dynamic Duo" on pages 208 and 209, measures 47–54 of "Reflections" on page 229, and the "intro" to letter B of "With All Due Respect" on page 195.)

3. a passage that includes a modulation. (See the interlude in "Group Effort" on page 175.)

Endings usually provide a heightened sense of finality. However, fade endings (which, in effect, are inconclusive) are also quite common. A typical example of a fade ending may be found in "Group Effort" on page 175.

In some cases, an ending will provide a bridge to a subsequent movement of a longer work. (See measures 269–277 of "Initiations" on page 227.)

Conclusive endings may be found in "With All Due Respect" (page 196), "Dynamic Duo" (page 210), "In Celebration of Saxophones" (page 200), and "This Is What We Do" (page 234).

The Arranger's Chorus

The arranger's chorus in a jazz arrangement presents an opportunity for the composer or arranger to **re**compose the original composition. In other words, in an arranger's chorus, the arranger becomes the improviser (on paper). During the big band era, the arranger's chorus came to be known as the "shout chorus" because it usually contained the climax to the arrangement.

An arranger's chorus usually follows the harmonic form of the original composition. A new melody, often resembling an improvised solo, is written over that form. Letter B of "Group Effort," which begins on the next page, is an arranger's chorus.

In longer compositions, the arranger's chorus may be replaced by a dramatic episode in which the composer provides one or more climactic moments. The form used may resemble that of previous sections, or it may be quite different. (See letter D of "Dynamic Duo," letter C of "Initiations," letter C of "Reflections," and letter E of "This Is What We Do.")

"Group Effort"

"Group Effort" is a short arrangement, for trumpet and tenor saxophone accompanied by piano, bass, and drums, of the (by now) familiar Beethoven melody from his Ninth Symphony. The format consists of an introduction, a melody chorus (letter A), an interlude based on two pedal points, an arranger's chorus (letter B), and a fade ending (coda). Other elements to observe include the change of key from Beethoven's original D major to F major (and later G major), two-part soli writing, counterpoint derived from guide tones, a modulation (processed in the interlude and realized at letter B), and constant structures over a pedal point (at B9).

Group Effort

Beethoven/arr. Pease

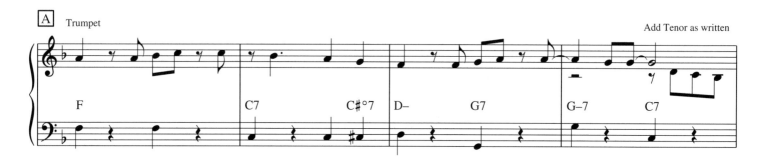

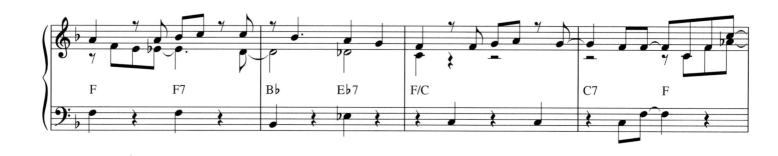

EXERCISES

Apply some or all of the following procedures to one of your original tunes.

1. Consider a four- to eight-measure introduction. How can you best set up your tune melodically, harmonically, and rhythmically?

2. After you state the tune, consider an interlude before beginning a solo section. Can the introduction be restated and serve as an interlude, or should there be new material? Can pedal point play a role?

3. Consider having a solo section. Will the solo form be the same as or different than the form of your tune?

4. Consider recomposing your tune in an arranger's chorus.

5. Consider the ending. Will your piece end with a sharp accent or a held chord? Will there be a fade ending instead?

Source Material

INTROS

Black Nile (Wayne Shorter)
Canteloupe Island (Herbie Hancock)
Firm Roots (Cedar Walton)
Groovin' High (Parker/Gillespie)
I Remember Clifford (Benny Golson)
Killer Joe (Benny Golson)
Morning (Clare Fischer)
New Girl (Duke Pearson)
Nica's Dream (Horace Silver)
Opus de Funk (Horace Silver)

INTERLUDES

New Girl (Duke Pearson)
Nica's Dream (Horace Silver)

ENDINGS

Groovin' High (Parker/Gillespie)
New Girl (Duke Pearson)
Nica's Dream (Horace Silver)

ARRANGER'S CHORUS

Along Came Betty (Benny Golson)
New Girl (Duke Pearson)
This Is for Albert (Wayne Shorter)
Whisper Not (Benny Golson)

CHAPTER 5
Metric Considerations

There is a reason why this chapter is titled "Metric Considerations" and not "Rhythmic Considerations." In effect, almost everything in our discussion of jazz composition so far has had something to do with rhythm: melodic rhythm, melodic rhythm density, motivic rhythm, motivic transformation, harmonic rhythm, etc. In short, rhythm has been an underlying theme in this text from the beginning. However, our discussion of rhythm in jazz would be incomplete without a mention of meter.

The roots of jazz—African rhythms, blues, ragtime, gospel, marches, work songs—all took hold in the fertile soil of duple meter. To this day, most jazz is written and played in 4/4 time with a swing feel. (Latin influences and fusion have added the option of subdividing the basic duple beat evenly.) Critics have sometimes suggested that this reliance on duple meter in jazz is a limitation, but most jazz musicians agree that 4/4 swing is the essential heartbeat of jazz.

Nevertheless, from time to time, jazz musicians have experimented with other time signatures. In the 1950s and 1960s, the jazz waltz became fashionable. Jazz waltzes such as "Bluesette" by jazz harmonica player Toots Thielemans and "Gravy Waltz" by bassist Ray Brown were popular examples. Pianist Bill Evans is still remembered for his recording of "Waltz for Debby."

Other time signatures began to pop up after Dave Brubeck's multi-metric album *Time Out* was issued. Paul Desmond's composition "Take Five" (in 5/4) and Brubeck's "Blue Rondo ala Turk" (in 9/8) quickly became jazz standards, and their opening ostinatos are still instantly recognizable. Indeed most jazz compositions in unusual meters rely on ostinatos for formal and rhythmic organization.

Don Ellis, a talented trumpet player and composer, fronted a big band in the 1960s that played music in many different and unusual meters including 5/4, 7/4, and 9/4. The title of his composition "33-222-1-222" represents the subdivision of the time signature of the piece, which is 19/8! The opening ostinato outlines the pulse subdivision.

In the 1970s and 1980s, fusion required not only a return to duple meter but also an even eighth-note subdivision of the beat because of its rock origins. Jazz purists still rail against this supposed corruptive influence, arguing in effect that "if it doesn't swing, it isn't jazz." (See chapter 6, "Fusion.")

Latin influences have also become pervasive in jazz: Afro-Cuban in the 1940s and 1950s, Brazilian (the bossa nova and samba) in the 1960s and 1970s, and Argentinean (e.g., the tangos of guitarist Astor Piazzolla) in the 1980s. Like fusion, these Latin genres are based mostly on duple meter. In addition, fusion and Latin styles often feature ostinatos as a central unifying element.

Contemporary jazz composers such as Chick Corea, Pat Metheny, Michael Brecker, and Billy Childs enjoy the challenges of writing and playing in unusual time signatures, often mixing them with straight-ahead passages in 4/4. One of the most interesting jazz compositions in recent years is "Escher Sketch" by Michael Brecker. The piece is written in 6/4 and alternates between the even eighth and sixteenth notes of rock and the swing eighth notes of jazz.

The musical examples that follow demonstrate 3/4, 5/4, and 7/4 respectively. "For Bill" (in 3/4) is written in *abac* song form. The melody is mostly diatonic to F Major, and the harmony is simple and functional. "Full House" is a blues based on an ostinato in 5/4. "Uno, Dos, Tres..." is a short through-composed modal piece in E Phrygian based on an ostinato in 7/4.

For Bill

Ted Pease

Full House

Ted Pease

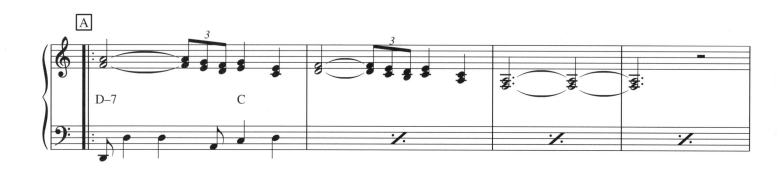

etc. repeat and fade

Uno, Dos, Tres...

Ted Pease

Metric Modulation

Metric modulation involves a change from one time signature to another. Examples of this include Chick Corea's "Tones for Joan's Bones" (metric modulation from 4/4 to 6/8 and back) and "Litha" (metric modulation from 6/8 to fast 4/4), and "How My Heart Sings" by Earl Zindars (metric modulation from 3/4 to 4/4 and back). Similar effects occur when there is a change of feel in the rhythm section. Some tunes, such as "Nica's Dream" and "Nutville" by Horace Silver and "A Night in Tunisia" by Dizzy Gillespie, change from a Latin feel to swing and back. In other tunes, such as "Whisper Not" by Benny Golson, there is a change from a "two feel" to "in four."

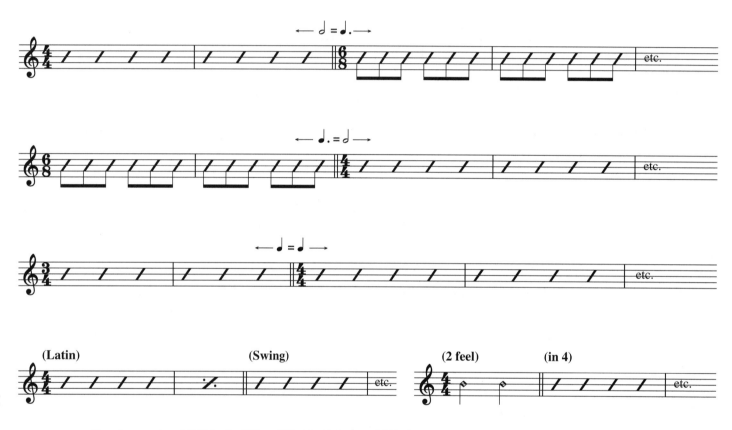

(See letter A of "This Is What We Do" (page 232) for examples of mixed meter.)

EXERCISES

1. Write a thirty-two-measure tune in 3/4 and in *abac* form.

2. Write a minor blues in 5/4 time.

3. Write a modal piece (choose any mode) based on an ostinato in 7/4.

4. Write a short through-composed composition that uses mixed meters.

5. Research the tunes referred to under "Metric Modulation." Find lead sheets and recordings whenever possible.

Source Material

3/4 (6/8, 6/4)

See "For Bill," page 179.
A Child Is Born (Thad Jones)
All Blues (Miles Davis) 6/8
At the Close of the Day (Fred Hersch)
Beauty Secrets (Kenny Werner)
Black Narcissus (Joe Henderson)
Blue Daniel (Frank Rosolino)
Bluesette (Toots Thielemans)
Blues for Yna Yna (Gerald Wilson)
Broken Wing (Richie Beirach)
Dark Territory (Marc Copland)
Dienda (Kenny Kirkland)
Dreams (Billy Childs)
Footprints (Wayne Shorter) 6/4
The Everlasting Night (Gary Willis)
Three Views of a Secret (Jaco Pastorius)
Up Jumped Spring (Freddie Hubbard)
Waltz for Debbie (Bill Evans)
West Coast Blues (Wes Montgomery)
Windows (Chick Corea)

5/4

See "Full House," page 180.
Exits and Flags (Milton Nascimento)
Take Five (Paul Desmond)

7/4

See "Uno, Dos, Tres...," page 181.
Little Wind (Geri Allen)
Miles Behind (Clare Fischer)
Willow (Paul McCandless)

MIXED METER

See "This Is What We Do," page 232.
The Beauty of All Things (Laurence Hobgood)
Blue Matter (John Scofield)
Dream On (Christophe Wallemme)
How My Heart Sings (Earl Zindars)
J Ben Jazz (Vinny Valentino)
Like Father, Like Son (Billy Childs)
Take Heart (Ralph Towner)
Trio Imitation (Kenny Werner)

CHAPTER 6
Fusion

A discussion of jazz composition would be incomplete without a mention of fusion. The influence of rock music on jazz and of jazz on rock first became noticeable in the music of younger musicians in the 1960s during the heyday of the Beatles. Vibraphonist Gary Burton, then in his twenties, led a quartet that included guitarist Larry Coryell, bassist Steve Swallow, and drummer Bob Moses. Burton's group began using rock as a stylistic element in some of its repertoire. Herbie Hancock, also in his twenties, used the even eighth notes and backbeat of rock on his albums such as *Maiden Voyage, The Prisoner,* and *Fat Albert Rotunda.* Freddie Hubbard used rock elements on his album *Red Clay.* Meanwhile, pop-rock groups such as Blood, Sweat & Tears and Chicago featured horn sections and incorporated extended jazz solos in many of their arrangements. There was give and take both ways.

In the late 1960s, Miles Davis became interested in the groove-oriented music of James Brown and in pop-rock bands such as Sly and the Family Stone. In a series of albums that included *Filles de Kilimanjaro* and *In a Silent Way,* and that culminated in the now classic *Bitches Brew,* Davis offered up an improvisational music based on ostinatos and rhythmic grooves that contained lengthy solo space and a minimum amount of formal composition. These albums became successively more electric with guitar and electric keyboard(s) becoming more and more prominent.

Participants in the *Bitches Brew* sessions included Joe Zawinul and Wayne Shorter, who subsequently formed Weather Report; Chick Corea, who later formed Return to Forever; John McLaughlin, who went on to form the Mahavishnu Orchestra; and Larry Young, who later played with drummer Tony Williams' group, Lifetime. That these fusion bands all seemed to descend from Miles Davis and *Bitches Brew* is probably the reason why many jazz historians cite *Bitches Brew* as the first true fusion album, even though the seeds of fusion were there long before that album came out.

For a while, there was something of an identity crisis in jazz. Jazz traditionalists complained that jazz-rock and fusion don't swing, and that electric instruments (other than perhaps hollowbody electric guitar) have no place in a true jazz band. Others argued that fusion cooks just as much as jazz, albeit at a slightly different temperature, and that it has introduced jazz to a broad spectrum of young rockers who otherwise might never have been exposed to it. In the final analysis, it is impossible to ignore a musical genre that essentially co-opted the jazz scene for more than twenty years. Other successful fusion practitioners in recent years have included Jeff Lorber, Pat Metheny, Lyle Mays, Russell Ferrante, Randy and Michael Brecker, John Scofield, and Aydin Esen.

So, what distinguishes fusion from bebop or post-bebop or modal jazz? One possible clue lies in who the writers of fusion are. Joe Zawinul, Chick Corea, Herbie Hancock, John McLaughlin, John Scofield, Pat Metheny, Lyle Mays, Jeff Lorber, Billy Childs, Aydin Esen, and Russell Ferrante (to name just a few) are all keyboard or guitar players. It is not surprising then that a lot of fusion composition is either keyboard or guitar oriented.

Fusion Melody

Melodically, there is a de-emphasis on the blues scale in fusion, unless the context is funk. Melodies are either mostly diatonic to major, minor, or modal scales, or they may occasionally (usually only momentarily) be intensely chromatic. Melodic rhythms move back and forth between notes of long duration (often tensions) that sustain over the rhythmic groove, and notes of shorter duration that move restlessly between the longer notes, often jabbing with syncopated attacks.

Fusion Harmony

Fusion harmony relies heavily on parallelism (constant structures), modal harmony, and chromatic harmony (chord progressions that are obtained by voice leading one or more notes of a chord by a half step to create a new chord—see below). There is a tendency in fusion to progress freely from chord to chord without necessarily pausing to confirm a particular tonality or modality. This can create surprisingly effective shifts in a progression, and final cadences can be delayed almost indefinitely for dramatic purposes. Voicings in fourths and fifths, and upper-structure triads and slash chords are common. Voicings in thirds are less common.

Parallelism (See "And There You Are," page 189, measures 29–30.)

Chromatic Harmony (See "And There You Are," page 189, measures 9–20.)

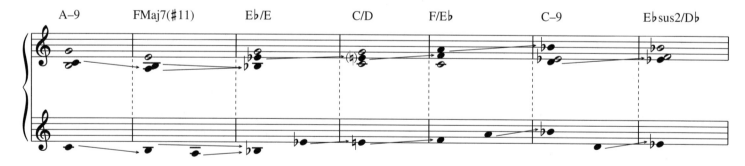

Funk/fusion dictates the use of dominant chords with blues-scale tensions, but "pure" fusion tends to de-emphasize the tritone and dominant chords in general. (If a dominant seventh chord does occur, it is usually in sus4 position.) Also absent (usually) are augmented, diminished, and half-diminished chords. Major seven and minor seven chords, liberally sprinkled with tensions, are much more prevalent. Fusion composers tend to avoid the idiomatic chord progressions of conventional jazz and bebop (II/V, secondary dominants, etc.).

Pedal point and ostinato are common in fusion tunes. And because fusion is rhythm-section oriented, the bass (sometimes doubled with keyboard and/or guitar) is often featured in the foreground either on the melody or on an important bass riff. When this happens persistently, I call it the "mega-bass" effect.

Fusion Rhythm

Most fusion is in duple meter (e.g., 4/4 or possibly 2/2) and features a persistent backbeat (this from its rock origins). Often there are Latin influences (especially Brazilian), and the use of Latin percussion is common. Some fusion composers (such as Chick Corea and Billy Childs) have used mixed meter (5/8, 6/8, 7/8, etc.) along with duple meter to good effect.

The walking bass lines of conventional jazz are noticeably absent. Bass lines in fusion tend to be just as syncopated as drum rhythms, and sometimes the bass line and the drum part are synchronized rhythmically. Whereas swing rhythms in jazz strive to be linear and smooth, fusion rhythms tend to be restless and often fragmented.

Fusion Instrumentation

The instrumentation of fusion bands is, by definition, electric and includes electric guitar(s), electric keyboard(s) (including synthesizers), and electric bass. The drums may be specially miked as well. There may be a wind instrument (usually a saxophone), and it too may be specially miked or hooked up to an electronic device such as an EWI (electronic wind instrument). Auxiliary percussion is also common.

The following tunes, "And There You Are," "Pedal to the Metal," and "With All Due Respect," are presented in a fusion context. "And There You Are" is a through-composed tune based on guide tones, a strong bass line, and chromatic harmony. If you follow the notes of long duration, you will discover its skeletal structure, which is illustrated on page 188.

The following sketch also shows the chromatic connections between the chords that allow the piece to visit distantly related tonal centers.

Sketch of "And There You Are"

Ted Pease

And There You Are

Ted Pease

If this tune sounds familiar, it's because you heard it earlier in a different context as the jazz ballad "Where Did You Go" (page 157).

"Pedal to the Metal" is in *aabb'ac* form. In the *a* section (measures 1–8), a bass line descends in half steps while inverted voicings in fourths harmonize a "melody" that descends in whole steps. In measures 7 and 8, triads harmonize an ascending melodic line while the bass descends chromatically. (The rhythms in measures 7 and 8 suggest a diminution of the rhythms in measures 2 through 4.) In the *b* section (measures 9–16), there is a four-measure conversation between the keyboard and the bass, followed in measures 13–15 by an echo of measures 2–4 in the keyboard part. In the *b'* section (measures 17–24), there is a sequence of measures 9–12 followed by another echo of measures 2–4, this time with an ascending melodic line. The *a* section then repeats and moves to the coda, where the *c* section of the form provides sustained chords against a pedal C and some drum fills.

The "changes" on the lead sheet to "Pedal to the Metal" are approximations of the harmonic content and are included for reference only. The piece is derived mostly from the bass line—chromatically restless in the *a* section, more melodic in the *b* and *b'* sections, and static in the *c* section.

Pedal to the Metal

Ted Pease

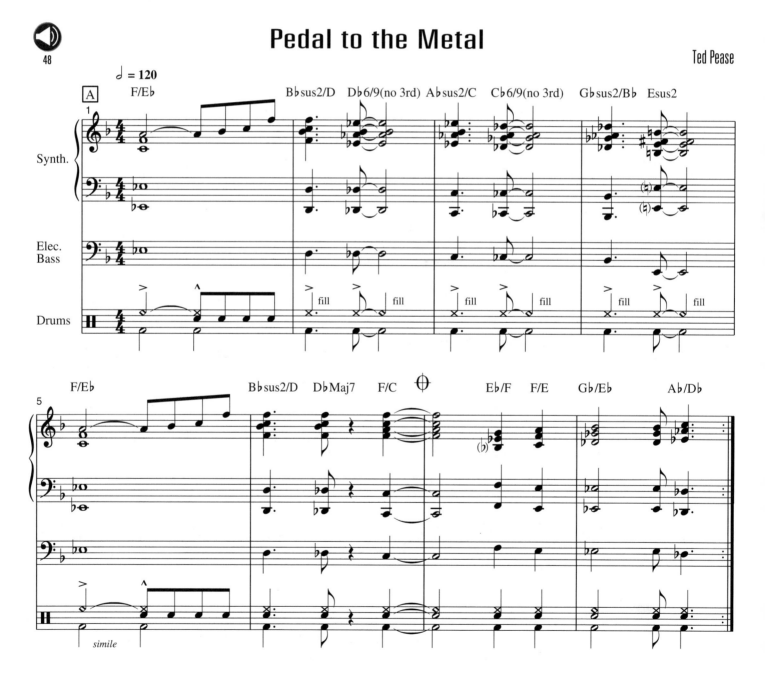

Solos

"With All Due Respect" is an episodic fusion composition with separate and distinct musical sections. The context is more funk oriented than the two previous pieces.

Intro (rubato piano solo)—emphasizes chromatic harmony against a melody in E minor that subsequently shifts to A minor

A section—piano vamp (based on the intro) establishes the tempo; theme is *aa'b* form (*b* recalls the intro)

B section—rhythmic ostinato (pentatonic-scale theme harmonized with constant structures)

C section—solo over B7 vamp utilizing the B7 symmetric diminished scale

D section—solo continues over intro changes (half-time feel); C section and D section played twice

E section—drum solo over B7 vamp

Recapitulation of the A section

Coda—emphasizes the B7 symmetric diminished scale; final eight measures recall the chromatic harmony of the intro and letter D

With All Due Respect

Ted Pease

Piano vamp continues ⟶

CHAPTER 7
Episodic Form

Episodic pieces have separate, complete sections that divide the whole of a piece into a series of self-contained musical units. The individual sections may contain important themes, changes in mood or tempo, or tonal or metric modulations. A given section may even contain its own separate song form or perhaps a blues form, and that form may be repeated as a basis for improvised solos. Examples of episodic jazz compositions include "Django" (John Lewis), "Three Views of a Secret" (Jaco Pastorius), "Spain" (Chick Corea), "Birdland" (Joe Zawinul), "Two Bass Hit" (Dizzy Gillespie), "Highland Aire" (Lyle Mays), and "Ecaroh" (Horace Silver).

Inasmuch as episodic forms contain separate and distinct musical units, we need to adjust the way we recognize and label them. Accordingly, we will use uppercase letters (A, B, C, etc.) for individual episodes, while we continue to use lowercase italicized letters (*a, b, c,* etc.) for any phrase subdivisions of those episodes. A hypothetical episodic piece might be laid out as follows:

> Introduction (eight measures—rubato, sets up F minor tonality)
> A (theme: sixteen measures at slow 4/4 tempo— *ab* form in F minor)
> B (new theme: thirty-two measures at slightly faster 4/4 tempo—*aba'* form in
>   B♭ major)
> C (new theme: twelve measures at fast 6/8 tempo—blues form in G minor; blues
>   form then repeated for solos followed by a recapitulation of the C theme to a
>   concluding fermata)
> A (recap of A theme)
> Coda

"In Celebration of Saxophones"

"In Celebration of Saxophones," which follows, is a short episodic piece in ABCA episodic form. Compare this piece to "Scrooge" (page 147), which is in *abca* song form. In "Scrooge," the *a, b,* and *c* sections are motivically similar. They are linked together by the common purpose of preparing the climax of the song in measure 21. The phrase lengths are symmetrical, and the whole tune stays close to the D minor tonality. The result is a thoroughly integrated thirty-two-measure "tune."

"In Celebration of Saxophones" is laid out differently. First, there is no rhythm section accompaniment. Second, the phrase lengths are different. The A section is a self-contained twelve-measure blues form. The B section is only eight measures long and contains an entirely new theme, first in B♭ minor and then (strikingly) in E major and D major, two key centers that are decidedly distant from the home key of D♭ major. The C section is in D minor and is also eight measures long. It contains another new theme, which is thoroughly diatonic but that creates some strong dissonances with triads against a chromatic bass line. The recapitulation of A relaxes the tension, and the extended coda contributes to the sense of impending finality. In the final analysis, the piece is experienced not as a tune (or "head") but as a collection of three different and yet integrated themes.

The scoring of the three different themes also helps to differentiate them. The alto saxophone plays the first theme, the baritone saxophone plays the second theme, and the tenor saxophone plays the third theme. The alto then returns to play the first theme again.

Form:

> A section—twelve-measure blues in D♭ major; alto solo
> B section—eight-measure theme in B♭ Aeolian and then E major and D major; baritone solo
> C section—eight-measure theme in D Aeolian; tenor solo
> A section—(dal segno al coda) repeat of the A section
> Coda—seven-measure concluding passage based on D♭ pedal point in the melody and chromatically descending dominant seventh chords in the harmony

Arranging and Scoring:

"In Celebration of Saxophones" contains a variety of three-, four-, and five-part voicing situations (designated as 3P, 4P, and 5P). The chorale style presents a unique challenge inasmuch as the scoring must provide a complete melodic, harmonic, and rhythmic soundscape without rhythm section accompaniment. The piece is scored for five saxophones: two altos, two tenors, and baritone. Because there are separate solos for alto, baritone, and tenor, much of the piece consists of melody with a three- or four-part background. Occasionally, all five horns come together to create a five-part texture. The following menu lists the various techniques as they occur measure by measure.

Measure(s)	Observe
1–2	alto solo with 4P spread background
3	3P voicings in 4ths; independent baritone
4	5P voicing includes melody as a separate fifth note
5–6	5P spread followed by four-way close (double lead 8vb)
7–8	alto melody with 3P spread background
9	5P spread voicing
10–12	alto melody with 3P spread background
13–15	baritone solo with 3P inverted 4ths background
16–20	5P variable voicings
21–23	tenor solo with 3P voicings in 4ths descending chromatically
24	tenor melody with 4P spread background
25–27	3P voicings (mostly upper structure triads) with an independent bass line that creates interesting slash chords
28	5P variable voicings
29–35(coda)	alto melody with 4P spread backgrounds

In Celebration of Saxophones

Ted Pease

Episodic pieces can employ a variety of musical blueprints that represent conceptual expansions of song form. Thus, it is not unusual to find episodic pieces in A B, A B C, A A B A, A B A C, or A B C A form. However, the episodes in such pieces are often longer (possibly even with subdivisions) and are decidedly more complete and independent than their song form counterparts. (For example, there may be modulations between episodes, as with "In Celebration of Saxophones.") In addition, portions of initial episodes may be revisited. For example, a piece that begins in A B A C episodic form might continue on to become A B A C B' A' C' A". The use of the apostrophe or the double apostrophe (A' or B' or C' or A") tells us that the essence of the preceding A, B, or C sections has been maintained, but certain alterations (change of key or mode, shortening, lengthening, motivic manipulation, reharmonization, etc.) have been employed to further develop the main idea.

EXERCISES

1. Listen to any or all of the following: "Django" (John Lewis), "Three Views of a Secret" (Jaco Pastorius), "Spain" (Chick Corea), "Birdland" (Joe Zawinul), "Two Bass Hit" (Dizzy Gillespie), "Highland Aire" (Lyle Mays), "Ecaroh" (Horace Silver). If possible, view lead sheets of these compositions. Identify the episodes in each. Determine whether any of the episodes have subdivisions and whether those subdivisions constitute a song form or the blues.

2. Using your through-composed tune, write an eight-measure interlude at the end of the tune based on a pedal point and a broken time feel in the rhythm section. Ideally, the interlude will also serve as an introduction to your tune. After the interlude, add an eight- to sixteen-measure repeating solo form based on a chord progression of four to eight chord changes that are not drawn from the main tune (use stretched out harmonic rhythms). A change in tonality or modality may be especially effective for the solo section. (The interlude may also suggest harmonic possibilities.)

   After the solo(s), write another interlude, similar to the first interlude but with some variation. Then develop the motivic material of your tune in an "arranger's chorus." Finally, write a coda based on the intro/interlude(s). The resulting form will be episodic: Intro; A section (your tune); interlude; B section (contrasting solo form); A' section (arranger's chorus); extended coda.

3. Write a short piece (two to four minutes) in ABCA episodic form for five horns without rhythm section. Use "In Celebration of Saxophones" as a model or devise your own blueprint.

Source Material—Episodic Compositions

Ana Maria (Wayne Shorter)
The Beauty of All Things (Laurence Hobgood)
Birdland (Joe Zawinul)
Celia (Charles Mingus)
Django (John Lewis)
Ecaroh (Horace Silver)
Little Wind (Geri Allen)
Lush Life (Billy Strayhorn)
Now He Sings Now He Sobs (Chick Corea)
Ode to the Doo Da Day (Jim Beard)
Reincarnation of a Lovebird (Charles Mingus)
Shawnuff (Charlie Parker/Dizzy Gillespie)
Spain (Chick Corea)
Straight Up and Down (Chick Corea)
Three Views of a Secret (Jaco Pastorius)
Time Track (Chick Corea)
When It Was Now (Wayne Shorter)

CHAPTER 8
Motivic Composition

Motivic composition presents a challenge to the jazz composer that is different from composing and/or arranging tunes. A motivic composition develops from one or more small musical fragments or "cells" instead of an integrated melody and chord progression, or "head," that is based on song form. Song forms are sometimes introduced as internal episodes in motivic compositions, but generally they tend to have supporting roles rather than serve as the central focus.

A motif usually consists of between two and eight notes, although circumstances may dictate something more extensive. It may be an interval, a broken chord, or some other short musical gesture lasting for a measure or two. A motivic composition is concerned with the manipulation and development of motifs. This manipulation and development is accomplished through the application of repetition, sequence, inversion, retrograde, retrograde inversion, displacement, harmonization, reharmonization, augmentation, diminution, truncation, modulation, and so forth.

The following exercises will give you some practice with motivic manipulation.

EXERCISES

Given the following motif and its scale (or harmonic) implications:

1. Derive four additional melodic variations using the given rhythm.

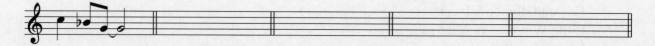

2. Derive four additional rhythmic variations using the given pitches.

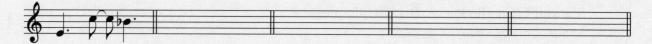

3. Derive eight additional harmonizations for the given motif.

4. Write a sixteen-measure melody using the given motif and similar variations.

Given the following motif and its scale (or harmonic) implications:

5. Derive five additional melodic variations using the given rhythm.

6. Derive five additional rhythmic variations using the given pitches. (Repeat notes if necessary.)

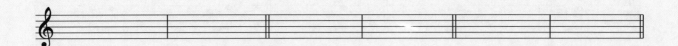

7. Derive ten additional variations using a combination of rhythms and pitches. Include embellishments if desired.

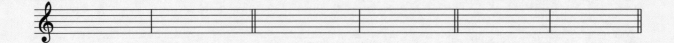

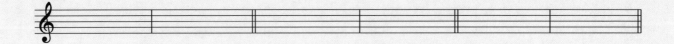

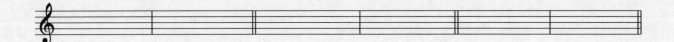

Internal Form for Motivic Compositions

The internal form involves the details of a piece. The internal form is where you try to find the delicate balance between familiar material (by way of motivic repetition or allusion) and new material (by way of tangents or variations) as the piece evolves. It is where you make decisions about tempo, style, tonality, modality, harmonic rhythm, consonance and dissonance, voicings, or counterpoint. It is where you decide whether or not to use recognizable internal episodes based on song forms or the blues to make your music more accessible to the players and audience. It is where you make decisions about orchestration. It is where you decide on solo forms and a host of other things. And it is where you will probably experience some moments of total exhilaration and other moments of total bewilderment and frustration. Such is the nature of the compositional process.

It helps to understand that you don't have to know all the details of a piece at the outset. Part of the process of composition involves letting go and letting a piece flow through you. You can't always plan for this; sometimes it just happens when you least expect it in the middle of the night or when you're on the bus. It is a good idea to keep a music sketchbook handy so you can jot down an idea before it "evaporates."

I find starting with an empty full-page score to be intimidating, so I always begin by using sketches on one, two, or three staves. I always begin simply, with a single brush stroke: a note, an interval, a chord, a "lick." If I like it, I might repeat it on the same, or perhaps a different, pitch axis. I am a fanatic about bass lines, so I try to be conscious of what is going to happen in the bass voice right away. (It may not be the string bass; it may be baritone saxophone, bass clarinet, or the left hand of the piano!)

The first four measures are usually the most difficult to conceive (although I have been lucky sometimes and have come to the writing desk with an idea firmly in mind). Once the first four measures are laid out, I usually try to develop those initial ideas for several measures. Hopefully, I will then have the makings of an A section, or at least an *a* subdivision of a gestating A section.

Confused about uppercase and lowercase letters? Remember that when an uppercase letter (A, B, etc.) is used in formal analysis, it refers to a complete episode, not the short phrase of a song form, as in *aaba* or *abac*, and not a portion of an episode. However, a complete episode of a longer composition (an A section, a B section, etc.) may contain subdivisions that can be defined with lowercase letters (*a, b, c,* etc.), whether those subdivisions represent song form or just contrasting musical ideas. (It should be noted that the beginning of an episode in a composition is often assigned an uppercase letter on the score and on the parts for rehearsal purposes. Subdivisions are usually labeled with just a measure number.)

To facilitate the creation of a *b* subdivision in the first A episode, I usually introduce a new motif. I often think of words with opposing meanings and try to find a way to express those opposites motivically. Word opposites like major/minor, tonal/modal, slow/fast, high/low, stable/restless, loud/soft, active/passive, treble/bass, or foreground/background can sometimes suggest musical direction.

Sometimes I connect the *a* and *b* subdivisions with a short interlude (four or eight measures). Turn to the next selection, "Dynamic Duo," and listen to the audio. Notice that the A section, which begins at measure 23, contains two subdivisions (labeled "a" and "b" on the score for descriptive purposes). The *a* and *b* sections are connected by a short interlude at measure 39.

Once you have an A section (with or without subdivisions) more or less the way you want it, there are several ways you can go:

1. Repeat the A section with orchestral variations and/or countermelodies. (If the variations are substantial, you may even consider this part the B section!)

2. Go into a holding pattern (an interlude) before proceeding, using a pedal point in the bass with motivic fragments over the top.

3. Further develop the A section using the usual techniques of sequence, inversion, retrograde, truncation, extension, augmentation, modulation, etc.

4. Begin the B section, which may consist of additional motivic development of the A section (e.g., in a different modal context), or the first solo, or perhaps a combination. For example, the solo may be accompanied by motivic references in the background.

5. Begin the B section with a completely new motif or theme.

6. Pause, go back, and create an intro to your piece that sets up the A section and that may have some use later as an interlude or coda (for example, an ostinato).

You can then continue to extend the form in many different ways:
- A, B, interlude, solos, etc.
- A, B, A, C, A, D, etc. (This is like classical rondo form.)
- A, B, interlude, then develop A more in a new tonality or modality and at a different pitch axis
- A, B, C, then develop B, then solo over an ostinato taken from the introduction, etc.

Eventually, you are going to want to bring the piece to a point of climax. (Indeed, there may be some mini-climaxes along the way.) The primary climax should occur approximately two thirds to three quarters of the way through. Following the climax there will probably be a recapitulation (return) to a portion of the initial material. There should be definite references to the original motivic material before you end the piece.

The internal form of "Dynamic Duo" is detailed in the next section. "Dynamic Duo" is a composition based on a descending half-step motif. The A and B sections are similar, but there is one significant difference based on these word opposites: foreground/background. In the A section, the trumpet and tenor are in the foreground as they play the main theme, while the rest of the ensemble plays a supporting role echoing the half-step motif in the background. In the B section, the ensemble is in the foreground as they play the main theme, while the trumpet and tenor play the supporting role echoing the half-step motif in the background. In other words, there is a reversal of roles.

The A and B sections both have *a* and *b* subdivisions. The C section contains solos for trumpet and tenor (the "Dynamic Duo") and backgrounds derived from the principal motivic material. The D section contains the primary climax following some contrapuntal layering of the main theme and the main motif. A recapitulation of the introduction and the B section follows, and a final chord with a motivic echo concludes the piece.

"Dynamic Duo"—Internal Form:

Measures 1–22: Introduction

1–4	loud ensemble chord
5–14	half-step motif stated by trumpet and tenor
15–22	piano plays half-step motif in augmentation to set up the A section

Measures 23–66: A section (Exposition)

subdivision *a*

23–30	main theme stated by trumpet and tenor; half-step motif echoed in turn by saxes, trumpets, and trombones
31–38	theme in melodic sequence; half-step motif echoed again
39–42	transition interlude

subdivision *b*

43–50	new triplet motif introduced with descending guide tones
51–54	triplet motif repeated with diminished chord arpeggio
55–58	concerted rhythm section figure answered by trumpet and tenor
59–68	piano plays half-step motif again to set up the B section

Measures 67–100: B section (Development)

subdivision *a*

67–74	main theme played by ensemble; half-step motif echoed by trumpet and tenor
75–82	theme in melodic sequence; half-step motif echoed again
83–86	transition interlude

subdivision *b*

87–92	triplet motif used with high target note
93–96	triplet motif with a different diminished chord arpeggio
97–100	concerted ensemble figure

Measures 101–150: C section (Further development with solos)

Measures 151–166: D section (Further development with climax)

151-162	contrapuntal layering of main theme and main motif
163–166	primary climax with loud ensemble chord (as in the intro) followed by D.S.

Measures 5–22 and 67–100: Abbreviated B section (Recapitulation)

Measures 167–169: Coda

167–169	final chord followed by final motivic response

Dynamic Duo

Ted Pease

EXERCISE

Develop a motivic composition in condensed two- or three-stave score format using one or more of the following motifs and the following blueprint:

1. At a minimum, include an A section of at least forty measures and a contrasting B section of at least twenty-four measures.

2. Use harmonic rhythms of two measures or longer in the A section and shorter harmonic rhythms and a different tonality or modality in the B section.

3. After the B section, write an interlude of at least eight measures based on a pedal point that leads to the first solo. (Use the same or a similar interlude leading to other solos.)

4. Derive solo changes from the A or B section, or use a totally different solo form. (Don't fall into the "head; solos on the head changes; repeat head" trap in this piece!)

5. Develop the piece further in a subsequent section that includes the primary climax. Include a modulation before or during this section.

6. Have a short recapitulation (do not use a D.C. or D.S.) of initial motivic material and conclude the piece with a satisfactory ending.

7. At some point, evaluate the need for an introduction.

8. Finally, decide how you might orchestrate your piece and get it played!

Source Material for Motivic Compositions

There are many excellent recorded examples of motivic jazz compositions available. Here is a short list:

"Ding, Dong, Ding" (Bob Brookmeyer) from *Mel Lewis and the Jazz Orchestra Play Bob Brookmeyer Compositions* (Gryphon G912)

"El Co"—1st movement (Bob Brookmeyer) from the same album

"Hello and Goodbye" (Bob Brookmeyer) also from the same album

"A Perfect Six" (Jim McNeely) from *Group Therapy* (Omnitone 15101)

"Real Life" (Jim McNeely) from *Real Life*, Phil Woods' Little Big Band (Chesky 47)

"Green Piece" (Maria Schneider) from *Evanescence* (Enja-8048 2)

"The Three Marias" (Wayne Shorter) from *Atlantis* (Sony COL 4816172)

CHAPTER 9
Extended Works

An extended work is not simply a long arrangement of a tune in standard theme-and-variations format. An extended work is to a tune what a novel is to a short story. In many instances, an extended work is an expanded episodic composition. There may be more than one movement, as in a suite. Each movement may have its own distinct flavor but still maintain a motivic or thematic connection to the whole. Programmatic pieces that are "about" something are also possible (for example, Duke Ellington's *Harlem*).

Duke Ellington was the first jazz composer to recognize the enormous possibilities for personal expression inherent in longer works. One of his early compositions, "Creole Rhapsody" (first recorded in 1931), is approximately six minutes long. "Creole Rhapsody" does not follow the standard theme-and-variations format of a traditional jazz composition or arrangement; instead, it features musical tangents alternating with a recurring theme. The form is similar to classical rondo form: ABACADAE, etc. Because of its length, "Creole Rhapsody" had to be recorded on both sides of a ten-inch 78 RPM record, something unprecedented for a jazz recording at that time. Ellington spent much of the rest of his life in the creation of significant extended jazz compositions such as *Diminuendo and Crescendo in Blue*; *Black, Brown, and Beige*; *Harlem*; and *The Sacred Concerts*. (Since the advent of long-playing records in the late 1940s, the three-minute time limit for jazz recordings no longer applies.)

Jazz history has produced other "serious" composers of note. In the 1940s, Stan Kenton's Orchestra provided a veritable music laboratory for the creation of so-called "progressive" jazz compositions by Pete Rugolo, Bob Graettinger, and Johnny Richards. Many jazz critics argued that because this really was "serious" music, it had no place in the jazz lexicon, particularly because there was a de-emphasis on improvisation and individual expression. Indeed, some of the music that Kenton recorded then sounded more like modern European classical music than jazz. In hindsight, it is clear that these composers were pushing the envelope and, along with Duke Ellington, arguing (musically) that jazz could be more than just syncopated dance music.

Similar criticism was leveled by some critics at the extended works of Third Stream composers such as Gunther Schuller, Charles Mingus, and George Russell in the 1950s and 1960s. But George Russell's composition *All About Rosie*, recorded in 1957, is generally regarded today as one of the most effective jazz compositions ever written.

Extended jazz works have become commonplace in recent years and are now accepted as a legitimate mode of expression by most jazz listeners. Below is a short list of some extended works in rough chronological order.

Composer	Composition	Album Title and Label
Duke Ellington	*A Tone Parallel to Harlem* (1951)	*Ellington Uptown* Columbia (CK 40836)
George Russell	*All About Rosie* (1957)	*Brandeis Jazz Festival* CBS SONY (25DP5327)
Thad Jones	*Central Park North* (1969)	*Complete Solid State Recordings of theThad Jones/Mel Lewis Orchestra* Mosaic (S25X-17929)
Claus Ogerman	*Symbiosis* (feat. Bill Evans) (1974)	*Symbiosis* Verve (314 523 381-2)
Chick Corea	*Tale of Daring* (1990)	*Inside Out* GRP (GRD-9601)
Maria Schneider	*Scenes from Childhood* (1996)	*Coming About* ENJA (ENJ-9069 2)
Bob Brookmeyer	*Celebration* (2000)	*New Works* Challenge Records (CHR 70066)

Motivic Continuity in Extended Works

The writing of an extended piece often begins with the smallest musical element: a motif. The motif may be an interval, a specific musical gesture (moving up or down), or a short thematic fragment. For example, Ellington's *Harlem* begins with a solo trumpet playing a descending minor third, which signifies the two syllables of the title.

This is similar to what happens in many classical compositions. A good example is this well-known motif from the Fifth Symphony of Beethoven.

We all know that opening statement, but we sometimes forget that most of what follows is derived from that opening motif.

Like Beethoven, many jazz composers use motivic development as a means of establishing variety and interest within longer works. A number of development techniques can be utilized in dealing with motivic ideas. Among them are repetition, sequence, inversion, truncation, extension, augmentation, diminution, and transformation. These techniques were introduced earlier in the discussion of through-composed tunes. (See pages 149–157.)

The accompanying audio includes *Suite for Jazz Band*, a three-movement jazz composition. The movements are titled "Initiations," "Reflections," and "This Is What We Do." The principal motif in the *Suite* is the following downward musical gesture:

The accompanying bass line is based on the inversion of the main motif:

Truncation, or foreshortening, is used toward the end of "This Is What We Do":

Extension, which involves a continuation of the motivic line, is also used toward the end of "This Is What We Do":

Diminution, which involves decreasing the note values of the motif, is used in "Reflections":

Augmentation, which involves increasing the note values of the motif, occurs toward the end of "Reflections":

Other devices that might have been used (but were not) include motivic transformation. (the rhythm of the motif can be retained while the pitch relationships change):

Motivic transformation can also accomplished by retaining the original pitch relationships while changing the rhythm (this was also considered, but not used):

Motifs can be subjected to harmonic variations. At the end of "This Is What We Do," a truncated version of the main motif is subjected to sequencing, extension, and reharmonization.

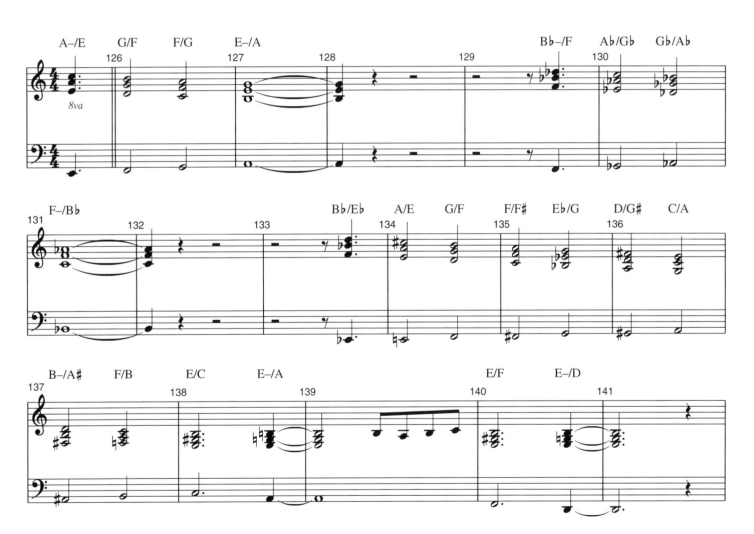

A motif can be orchestrated in a variety of ways. The principal motif is heard several times in "Initiations," the first movement of the *Suite*. First, it is presented by solo piano:

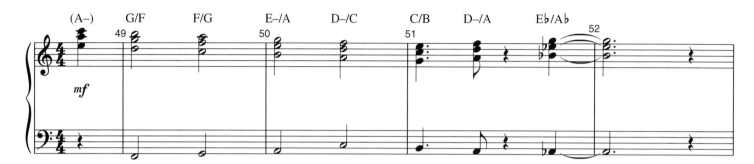

Next, it is heard in a soli passage for five saxophones:

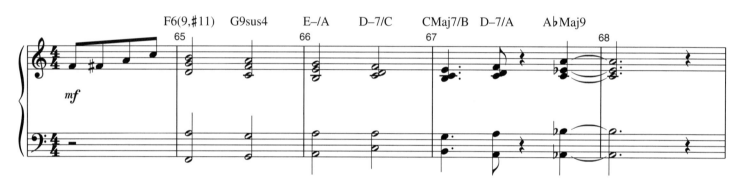

Next, it is heard in an ensemble tutti:

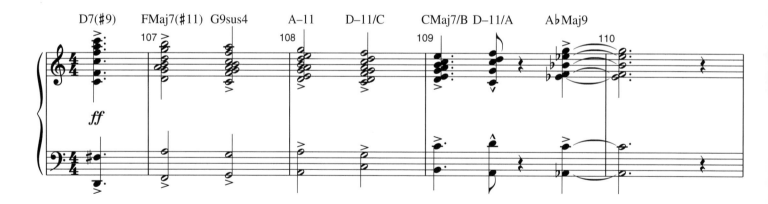

At the end of "Initiations," it is scored for the brass with a counterpoint in the saxophones:

In "Reflections," the second movement of the *Suite*, the motif is presented in a minor key by soprano saxophone.

Later in the same movement, the motif is scored for the brass section.

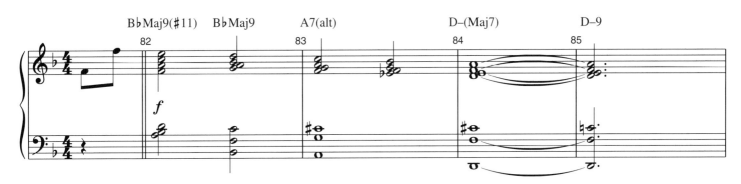

In "This Is What We Do," the third movement of the *Suite*, the motif is scored once
again for the full ensemble with some added dissonance.

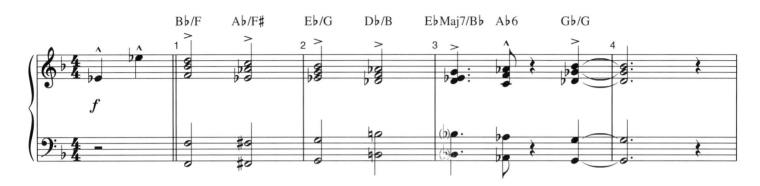

Sometimes, as we have seen with through-composed tunes, a complete song form can be
generated from an initial motif. In "Reflections" there is a sixteen-measure theme that
contains references to the main motif. First, the main motif is heard in diminution
in measure 1. In measures 5 and 6 the main motif is inverted. In measures 7 and 8 there
is a sequence of that inversion. The main motif is heard one more time in measures 13
and 14.

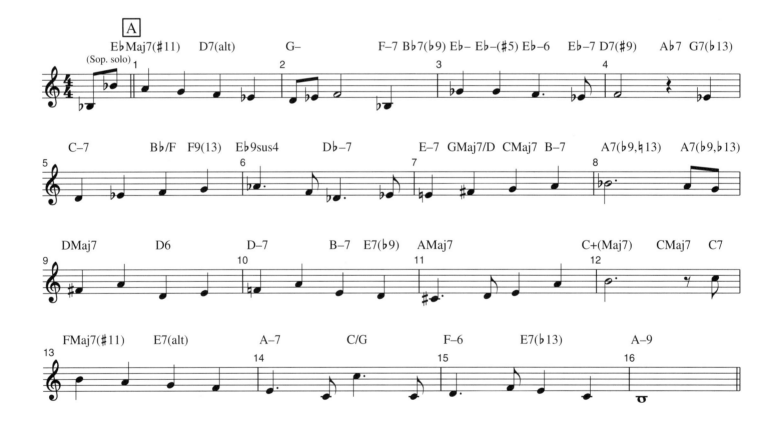

There are other important motifs in the *Suite*. There is the "mega-bass" motif that occurs prominently at the beginning of "Initiations." This motif is also used as raw material for the *b* section of the main theme at measure 79.

A thematic motif appears at the beginning of the main theme of "Initiations" at measure 41:

Earlier, there is an allusion to the thematic motif in measures 28–30 (via motivic transformation):

There is also the intervallic motif of the perfect fifth that can be heard throughout "Initiations" in various settings:

External Form for Extended Works

The external form is the overall blueprint or broad outline of an extended piece. The foregoing music examples from *Suite for Jazz Band* are isolated snapshots from a larger musical panorama. Indeed, some of these examples came from a sketchbook I kept during the initial stages of composing the piece. These and other examples had to be placed in a larger context as the architecture of this extended work took shape.

The external form of an extended piece can usually be described verbally. *Suite for Jazz Band* might be described as follows:

I. "Initiations": medium-fast swing tempo. Main motivic material introduced and developed. Trumpet solo featured. Full orchestration in dialog with the trumpet toward the end of the movement. Inconclusive ending suggesting the full piece has more to come.

II. "Reflections": slow rubato evolving to easy Latin tempo. Motivic material used to build a through-composed theme for soprano saxophone. Full orchestration of portions of the theme support soprano jazz.

III. "This Is What We Do": fast swing tempo. Motivic material reintroduced and transformed rhythmically, harmonically, and orchestrally. Solos by soprano saxophone, trombone, and trumpet. Primary climax of the piece occurs toward the end with full orchestration. Conclusive ending.

This outline is similar to classical concerto form (although it features more than one soloist): the first movement (allegro) is bright and peppy, the second movement (adagio/andante) is the "slow" movement, and the third movement (presto) is fast and exciting. I didn't use those classical tempo designations, but the intent was the same.

A variety of external forms is available to the jazz composer. The most common form is the suite. Early suites in classical repertoire were multi-movement compositions based on dance forms. Later, the suite became an extended episodic instrumental form with separate sections or movements based on an even larger work, such as an opera or a ballet. *The Nutcracker Suite* by Tchaikovsky is an example of the latter. Jazz composers use the suite form to express a variety of musical impressions about some central idea or thing. Duke Ellington's *Harlem* is a good example. It covers a broad range of musical impressions in separate and distinct episodes about the African-American community in New York City.

The concerto is another extended form also favored by jazz composers, although that actual term is rarely used. Just as in classical music, the jazz concerto features a single performer with ensemble accompaniment. *Symbiosis* by Claus Ogerman features pianist Bill Evans with a large orchestra. *Focus* by Ed Sauter features tenor saxophonist Stan Getz with a string orchestra.

Another common treatment of form in extended jazz compositions can best be described as "free rhapsody" or "fantasy." (Again, these actual terms are rarely used by jazz composers.) In effect, the composer moves through the piece free of any specific formal design, although clear motivic and/or thematic references may appear from time to time to supply focus.

How do you know what external form an extended piece is going to take before you start? That question breeds other questions: Will the piece be in one, two, three, or more movements? Does the piece have programmatic content—is it about a person, a place, an event? What tempos and styles should be represented in the piece? Are there requirements for the piece that are dictated by a commission or a grant proposal or a class assignment? Are you writing the piece with a particular ensemble in mind? Will the piece feature a particular performer or performers? Approximately how long is the piece going to be?

It helps to know the answer to some, if not all, of these questions before you begin. Otherwise, the task may seem overwhelming. In my case, I had a pretty good idea of what the external form was going to be because I had to give a broad description of the proposed work in a grant proposal to the National Endowment for the Arts. I knew the piece was going to be in more than one movement and that it would be motivic and episodic. I also knew that I wanted to include substantial solo space for several players on relatively simple solo forms.

Sometimes, a composer will begin a piece without knowing what the length will be or anything else. Sounds may be filling the composer's head, and the impulse to write *anything* is too strong to resist. This is actually an exciting, if somewhat scary, feeling. It goes with the territory. Duke Ellington was famous for saying that his favorite piece was "the next one." Words to live by!

Internal Forms for Extended Works

A variety of internal forms may be used in an extended work.

1. One of the most common internal forms is the blues. For example, Ellington's *Harlem* makes significant use of the blues in the middle of the overall work.

2. Song forms, such as *aaba* and *abac*, are sometimes used as episodes in longer works. Ellington's extended work *Black, Brown, and Beige* contains the beautiful *aaba* song "Come Sunday" as one of its movements. "Reflections" is a sixteen-measure through-composed song form.

3. Rondo form is featured in Dave Brubeck's composition "Blue Rondo à la Turk" which, although he may not have intended it that way, is the first "movement" from his and Paul Desmond's "suite," *Time Out*, the common musical thread of which is the exploration of unusual time signatures.

4. Another common internal form used in extended works is theme and variations. "Initiations" uses theme and variations (with a few extensions) beginning at letter A. "Reflections" features soprano saxophone on a theme and variations. (*Suite for Jazz Band* is heard as a single extended work because of all the motivic references.)

5. Sometimes, composers will borrow from themselves in a piece. The opening episode of "This Is What We Do" is borrowed from "Reflections." (The melody and harmony of "Reflections" are transformed rhythmically.) Also, the final section of "This Is What We Do" beginning at measure 118 is borrowed from "Initiations."

A composer sometimes has to "step back" from a piece to get a sense of how the form is evolving. One method I have suggested to students is to write short, eight-measure verbal summaries of their pieces on a bunch of 3x5 cards so as to represent the piece in miniature. They then can lay these cards out on a table or the floor in order to see where they have been and, hopefully, where they are going. This method helps in discovering (a) the proportions of a piece, (b) whether or not a section might need to be repeated, (c) whether solos are introduced too soon, (d) whether an ending is too abrupt, or (e) where the piece has taken a left turn into a blind alley. (This method is less cumbersome than laying out full-size score paper!)

Suite for Jazz Band
This composition was written with the support of the National Endowment for the Arts.

I. "INITIATIONS"

Internal Form:

Measures 1–40: Introduction

1	initial exclamatory chord
3–5	"mega-bass" motif stated by bass and baritone sax
13–15	"mega-bass" motif on different pitch axis
21–23	"mega-bass" motif on different pitch axis
29–30	allusion to main theme motif (to be introduced at meas. 41)
33–40	piano sets up main theme

Measures 41–118: A section (Exposition)

41–72	part *a* of main theme (contains principal motif)
73–78	interlude
79–98	part *b* of main theme (contains "mega-bass" motif)
99–118	part *a* of main theme restated

Measures 119–190: B section (Development)
trumpet solos on 72-measure elongated *aaba* form with ensemble backgrounds

Measures 191–260: C section (Further development with climax)

191–222	trumpet and ensemble trade "8s"
223–242	trumpet solos on *b* changes
243–254	ensemble passage leading to primary climax at 251
255–260	trumpet vamps

Measures 261–277: Coda

261–268	restatement of "mega-bass" motif
269–277	trumpet vamps until final chord

Initiations

Ted Pease

Suite for Jazz Band

II. REFLECTIONS

Internal Form:

Measures 1–16: A section (Exposition)
        1–16 soprano saxophone and piano present a theme drawn from the principal motif of the *Suite* in rubato style
        16–19 tempo established

Measures 20–47: B section (Development)
        20–35 soprano solo on chord changes from the theme in augmented harmonic rhythm (twice the original value)
        36–46 soprano solo continues on chord changes from the theme in the original harmonic rhythm

Measures 47–54: Interlude
        47–54 soprano vamps on F+Maj7 while rhythm section builds toward the modulation at letter C

Measures 55–77: C section (Further development with climax)
        55–62 ensemble passage over changes in augmented harmonic rhythm
        63–70 sax soli over changes in augmented harmonic rhythm; primary climax reached in measure 69
        71–77 soprano solo on remaining changes from the theme in original harmonic rhythm

Measures 78–93: Coda
        78–81 soprano vamps over tonic minor chords in E minor and D minor
        82–85 brass play principal motif in augmented rhythm
        86–89 trombones echo the principal motif in augmented rhythm
        90–93 soprano plays principal motif in augmented rhythm

Reflections

Ted Pease

Detail of "Reflections" sax soli at measure 63:

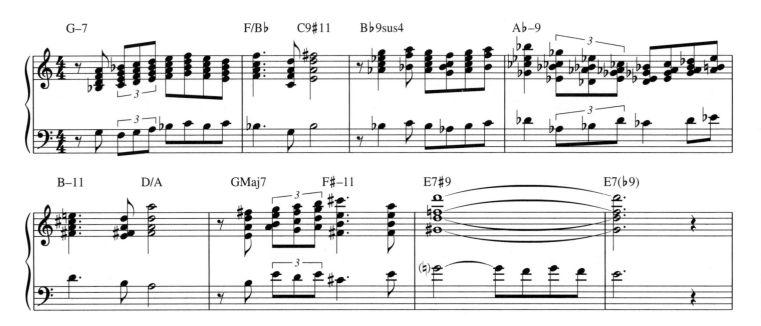

Suite for Jazz Band

III. THIS IS WHAT WE DO

Internal Form:

Measures 1–43: A section (Exposition)
> This section restates the theme from "Reflections" in somewhat disguised fashion through the use of dissonant reharmonizations and metric modulations to 3/4 that produce dramatically augmented melodic rhythms alternating with drum fills.

Measures 44–59: B section (soprano solo)
> Soprano saxophone repeats the role of soloist on changes that are derived from the changes to "Reflections."

Measures 60–77: C section (trombone solo)
> The trombone solo takes off from the syncopated rhythm in the last two measures of the soprano solo (recurring accent on beat 4).

Measures 78–117: D section (trumpet solo)
> The trumpet returns to solo on the changes to "Initiations."

Measures 118–145: E section (Recapitulation and primary climax)
> 118–125 recapitulation of the theme from "Initiations"
> 126–141 recapitulation of the principal motif of the *Suite* using truncation, reharmonization, and extension (see detail on page 217)
> 142–145 drum solo

Measures 146–157: Coda
> 146–147 pyramid
> 148–155 trumpet, soprano, and trombone "jam it up"
> 155–157 final chord with trumpet exclamation point on top

This Is What We Do

Ted Pease

EXERCISE

Develop an extended work in three movements in the following stages:

1. What instrumentation will you be using?

_____

_____

_____

_____

2. Plan the external form. Use a general verbal description.

I. First movement
   approximate length (in minutes):_____
   tempo:_____
   meter or groove: _____
   tonality or modality:_____
   featured soloist(s):_____

II. Second movement
   approximate length (in minutes):_____
   tempo:_____
   meter or groove: _____
   tonality or modality: _____
   featured soloist(s):_____

III. Third movement
   approximate length (in minutes):_____
   tempo:_____
   meter or groove: _____
   tonality or modality:_____
   featured soloist(s):_____

3. Determine the principal motif(s):

4. Begin a sketchbook sketch and let the piece begin to flow through you.

Bibliography

The following legal fake books were consulted for analysis of individual tunes and for the compilation of source material lists for individual chapters.

Hal Leonard Corporation, 7777 W. Bluemound Rd., Milwaukee, WI 53213
    The Ultimate Jazz Fakebook (Compiled by Dr. Herb Wong), 1988

Sher, Chuck (Publisher and Editor). Sher Music Co., P.O. Box 445, Petaluma, CA
    The World's Greatest Fakebook, Copyright 1983.
    The New Real Book, Copyright 1988.
    The New Real Book (Volume 2), Copyright 1991.
    The New Real Book (Volume 3), Copyright 1995.
    The All-Jazz Real Book, Copyright 2001 (includes CD).
Note: *The All-Jazz Real Book* contains an excellent CD that features a number of the selections presented in the book. All of the Sher books contain complete discographies that are extremely helpful in locating definitive recordings of individual tunes.

The following books have been in my music library for a long time. Although their purview is primarily "classical" music, they have helped to provide blueprints in style and substance for the content of this book.

Dallin, Leon. *Techniques of Twentieth Century Composition*. Dubuque, Iowa: Wm. C. Brown Company, 1968.

Persichetti, Vincent. *Twentieth Century Harmony*. New York: W.W. Norton and Co., 1961.

Salzer, Felix. *Structural Hearing*. New York: Dover Publications, 1982.

In addition to being an excellent reference work on the history and evolution of jazz arranging, the following book provides models of layouts for longer works that I was able to adapt in the presentation of extended works.

Sturm, Fred. *Changes Over Time: The Evolution of Jazz Arranging*. Advance Music, 1995.

Suggested Reading

Davis, Miles. *The Autobiography*. Simon and Schuster, Inc., 1989.

Easton, Carol. *Straight Ahead: The Story of Stan Kenton*. Da Capo., 1973.

Ellington, Duke. *Music Is My Mistress*. Doubleday, 1973.

Evans, Gil. Joe Muccioli, Jeff Sultanof, editors. *The Gil Evans Collection: 15 Study and Sketch Scores from Gil's Manuscripts*. Hal Leonard Corporation, 1997.

Gillespie, Dizzy and Al Fraser. *To Be or Not To Bop: Memoirs*. Doubleday, 1979.

Gitler, Ira. *From Swing to Bop*. Oxford University Press, 1985.

Hajdu, David. *Lush Life: A Biography of Billy Strayhorn*. North Point Press, 1996.

Hasse, John. *Beyond Category: The Life and Genius of Duke Ellington*. Da Capo Press, 1995.

Khan, Ashley. *Kind of Blue: The Making of the Miles Davis Masterpiece*. DaCapo Press, 2000.

Kernfeld, Barry, ed. *The New Grove Dictionary of Jazz*. St. Martin's Press, 1994.

Litweiler, John. *Ornette Coleman: A Harmolodic Life*. Wm. Morrow, 1993.

Lowell, Dick and Ken Pullig. *Arranging for Large Jazz Ensemble*. Berklee Press, 2003.

Lyons, Len. *The 101 Best Jazz Albums: a History of Jazz on Record*. Wm. Morrow, 1980.

Mingus, Charles. *Beneath the Underdog: His World as Composed by Mingus*. Penguin, 1980.

Pease, Ted & Pullig, Ken. *Modern Jazz Voicings*. Berklee Press, 2001.

Pettinger, Peter. *Bill Evans, How My Heart Sings*. Yale University Press, 1998.

Porter, Lewis. *John Coltrane, His Life and Music*. University of Michigan Press, 1998.

Schuller, Gunther. *The Swing Era*. Oxford University Press, 1990.

Van De Leur, Walter. *Something to Live For: The Music of Billy Strayhorn*. Oxford University Press, 2002.

Wright, Ray. *Inside the Score*. Kendor, 1982.

0214